KU-686-734

Contents

Introduction

Curriculum vitae literally means 'course of one's life', so your CV, or resumé, is designed to show just that. It is a synopsis of your education, your work or career history, job training, skills, knowledge and abilities. Common usage has made this document an essential tool in today's competitive job market. An effective CV is a key element in your search for the job you want. Your CV should help you market yourself, highlight your skills, promote your knowledge and experience, and describe your ability and personality. This guide will help you to create a CV to do just that.

Whether you are applying for your first job or moving on in your career, a good CV is essential. Most people change jobs, and sometimes careers, several times in their working lives, and this will become increasingly the case in the 21st-century job market. A well-written, carefully constructed CV is an essential tool if you are going to succeed in successfully applying to your chosen company or organisation.

When you apply for a job, you may be competing with dozens, if not hundreds, of applicants. The first thing an employer will want to do is to reduce those numbers to something more workable, so first impressions count. Yours has to be one of the CVs that catch their eye right from the start. It should be accessible, well-presented, targeted to the job on offer and full of potential benefit to their company. They are likely to have time only to read each one quite quickly; so yours must stand out and be one of the ones selected for further investigation.

write your CV - get the job

essentials

lesleen edwards

foulsham
LONDON · NEW YORK · TORONTO · SYDNEY

foulsham
The Publishing House, Bennetts Close,
Cippenham, Slough, Berks, SL1 5AP, England

ISBN 0-572-03028-2

A CIP record for this book is available from the British Library

Printed in Great Britain by Cox & Wyman Ltd, Reading

Once the selected CVs have been analysed in detail, they will be assessed against the job description by two or three people, or even a panel of selected general and management staff, depending on the vacancy, in order to select a handful of applicants for interview. To keep you in the running, your CV has to show the right depth of knowledge and experience, with a personality profile that makes you a great candidate.

For most job applications, your CV and covering letter will be the only source of information for a potential employer who is trying to create a picture of the person he or she wants to join the firm. It is, therefore, impossible to overestimate its importance in helping you to win the opportunity of that all-important interview. So it's certainly worth investing time and effort into getting it right. Whatever you have to offer, if you work through the steps outlined in the following chapters, you will be able to present yourself in a positive and professional way.

This guide will help you to identify your skills and abilities and present them in the best possible light. It will give you guidance on how to define your aims and ambitions, and show you how to include them to your best advantage in your application. Assessment of the job on offer and how to target your application to the specific job requirements is also important, so the guide will show you how to examine and understand job advertisements so you know what the company is looking for and understand how to present your CV in order to reflect the demands of the job. Plus, there are tips and examples on the most effective layout and structure.

You will find examples of CVs for various jobs and for different types of personal situation, including applying for your first job, looking for a promotion or a change of direction, returning to work after a break, and seeking work after retirement.

You will also need to write covering letters and fill in application forms, so we include full information on how to make those important documents count.

Of course, when your CV and letters succeed and you are offered that vital interview, you'll need guidance regarding interview technique and Chapter 17 has some great tips on how to perform well at the interview.

So with success as the goal, let's start work on putting together the CV that is going to get you the interview, and the interview that is going to get you the job.

Chapter 1

Getting Started – the Basics of CV Writing

In this first chapter, I am going to give an overview of what a CV is for, what it should contain and how to present the information. This should help you to define the objectives you need to achieve and set you thinking about how you are going to reach them. The following chapters will then go into more detail on each section, with plenty of examples to help you construct your own effective CV.

As competition for the best jobs becomes increasingly fierce, the need for a good CV becomes ever more important. When you are applying for a job, it is your CV that will get you through the first screening – or trip you up at that first hurdle. It's the only thing that opens the door to that crucial interview – or slams it in your face! It hardly needs saying, therefore, that it is worth working really hard to make sure your CV gives an accurate but hard-hitting and effective picture of your qualities. It will take time and effort, but that will be rewarded.

A CV is not a place for modesty. It is tool to help you to get the job you want. An effective CV will tell a prospective employer that you have the necessary skills, knowledge and commitment to do the job you are applying for, and that you have the right attitude and personality to fit in with the company image and with the other employees. It should be a complete snapshot of you at your most photogenic!

An effective CV must be concise, easy to read, and relevant to the job you are applying for, and give the reader a clear picture of your experience and achievements. It should persuade the employer to mark you out as a short-list candidate for their interview list. You therefore need to make every word count. In order to make it easy for the potential employer to access the information they want, it makes sense to write your CV in easy-to-read sections, each one with a tightly defined purpose and clear structure and organisation.

When do you need a CV?

There will be many occasions when you will need your CV and, once you have constructed it, you should review it regularly to make sure you keep it up-to-date. It is worth doing this even if you are not job-hunting as it will make it much easier to update and much more accurate when you do need it.

You can use a CV in various ways:
- At careers fairs when you want to leave your details with employers.
- To send to an employer when you are writing a speculative letter about possible employment.
- To accompany an application when a CV is requested.
- To give to an employer at interview if they have not seen your details.

If an employer asks you specifically to fill in an application form, that may be a nuisance after you have spent time on your CV, but don't be tempted just to send the CV anyway; do what they have asked. You will be able to use all the information on your CV to fill in the form.

Where to start

There are lots of elements to a CV and you will need to draft and re-draft, add information and modify it, so working on a PC is the perfect way to work on your CV because you can keep improving it as often as you like. At the risk of stating the obvious, always keep an up-to-date print-out and a disk back-up just in case.

I suggest you start with a basic word-processing document containing just the facts and information, and work on that until you are happy with what it contains. The following chapters will take you in detail through each individual section. Once you have done that, you can start thinking about format and presentation, which we'll deal with in Chapter 11.

Open a new A4 document on your PC, either as an ordinary document or as a table. Use a common word-processing program, such as Word, so that you can easily send your CV as an e-mail attachment, if requested, and be sure that the employer will be able to access the document easily. Set up uniform margins at about 2.5 cm and select a clear and classic font in 12pt size with single spacing. Then you are ready to start.

Jot down words, phrases and expressions in each category that you think might be useful. Check up on dates, names and addresses so that you have the bare bones. Once you have all the source information you need in each section, set about refining the information into bullet points or text.

You will also find it helpful to read some job advertisements, including advertisements in publications relevant to the type of work you are looking for. The descriptive words used by employers will tell you what abilities they are looking for and could help you find the right words or phrases for your own application.

What a CV should contain

An effective CV is built up around well-thought-out, clearly headed, easy-to-read sections. To make every word count, it is worth spending time getting each section right. This is an overview: The following chapters work on each section in detail with tips to guide you, and helpful examples relevant to each section.

By definition, all CVs are unique, but they do follow the basic structure outlined here. However, there will always be sections that don't apply to you, or other sections that you need to expand or sub-divide. Always remember that this is *your* CV so just keep in mind the purpose of the document and adjust it in any way you think will give you that edge over the other candidates.

Don't make the mistake of thinking that you have to include every detail of your life on your CV; you only need to include things that are relevant to your employment prospects. At the start, include all such relevant information. Once you are tailoring your basic CV to a specific job (see Chapter 10 on page 60), you may make some finer adjustments.

Ordering the sections

The order in which the sections are presented usually follows the example sequence shown on page 13, but if you feel that your skills and experience are best conveyed by changing the order of the sections, then do so, although the personal section should always come first. You may, for example, have extensive language skills from travelling or living in another country, and feel you want to draw the attention of a multi-national company to that fact before you detail less directly relevant educational qualifications.

Your first CV

If you are applying for a job direct from full-time education, an employer will obviously not be able to gauge anything from a career history. It is therefore particularly important that you include other information that will tell the employer more about you, such as relevant work experience, any special schemes you have participated in such as the Duke of Edinburgh Award, and vacation or voluntary work you may have done. From these activities, the prospective employer will be able to note whether you have any experience in a working environment, of following instructions and working to a predetermined standard; whether other people regard you as responsible, hard-working, punctual, reliable, self-reliant, motivated – and so on. Therefore, include qualities which allow you to demonstrate what a good employee you would make.

Unusual circumstances

If you have an unusual career history, have had an employment break, have changed or are trying to change career direction, or perhaps have been a mature student and are bringing new qualifications to your employment, you may need to do some extra work on your CV and change it from the basic pattern outlined on page 13. You will still need to include fundamental information, but you will find more specific guidance in Chapter 9 (see page 55) on how to ensure your CV is as effective as it can be.

Length

At this stage, don't worry too much about how much information you are going to include because you will have plenty of time to refine and improve it. Eventually, however, you will be looking to create a CV that is about two pages long, so keep that in mind if you have a tendency to be convoluted. Exceptions to this rule would be if an employer has specifically asked for a one-page CV or, if you are in the medical profession for example, where CVs tend to be longer than two sides of A4.

You should try to keep to the expected length, as it will allow you to include all the information that is relevant to the job application without overloading the employer with unnecessary information; that will only give him or her the impression that you cannot prioritise. If your CV is too short, on the other hand, it will look as though you have nothing to interest the employer.

Page one usually deals with your personal details and education and at least some of your work experience. Page two continues with work details, then covers your skills, interests and references.

Chronology of information

It used to be the case that each section of the CV listed details in chronological order; this is why you will still see some CVs constructed in this way. However, since the most important thing to an employer is your highest skill levels and what you have achieved most recently, it is

Example outline

Personal details
Personal and contact information including: name, address, telephone number, e-mail and so on.

Personal profile
A concise descriptive statement of who you are, what you have achieved to date and what you hope to achieve.

Education and training
Your educational background, including academic and professional qualifications.

Career history
An outline of your work experience, capabilities and key achievements.

Special skills and abilities
Any additional qualifications and achievements relevant to the application.

Interests and activities
Leisure interests and hobbies designed to give a fuller picture of your personality.

References
Responsible referees who will support your application.

now standard practice to put the most recent details first and work backwards. This obviously becomes increasingly important as you progress in your career. Always be consistent – don't do one section chronologically and the next in reverse.

Your focus should also be on the most recent information. If you give a great deal of detail of what you did ten years before, the employer might think your recent experience is of little value.

Text presentation

Since space is likely to be at a premium, write concisely. Since communication is crucial, write clearly and simply. Avoid jargon and clichés. Use technical terminology only where it is relevant, not in an attempt to sound impressive.

Some CVs are written in a prose style – brief paragraphs of text – and others are presented as bullet points. Both are perfectly valid. Prose allows for more subtlety of detail, whereas bullet points are easier to scan and extract the most vital information. It is up to you to choose the style that allows you to communicate your skills most effectively. You may choose to use bullet points for some sections – qualifications and interests, for example – but use a more detailed prose style for your work experience and skills.

Specific details and evidence

Keep in mind that you need to be clear and specific with all the information you include, especially when you come to the personal qualities and interests that will help the employer to get a picture of your personality. It is easy to list GCSE or A level subjects and grades from which the employer can gain a clear idea of your educational qualifications. However, when you come to describe the tasks you have done in a job, the responsibilities you have undertaken, or perhaps your hobbies, you need to be as specific as possible. You may know that you were the Managing Director's right hand as his PA, dealing with everything from organising the office to structuring a conference, but don't forget 'estate-agent syndrome' – some people may refer to themselves as a 'PA' when what they actually mean is 'secretary' or even 'typist'. Each job has its own skills and qualities but they are not the same, so be forthcoming with details of what your job actually entailed, so that an employer can gauge what your skills really are. Similarly, if you put 'sport' as one of your interests, it could mean anything, whereas 'play rugby for 3rd XV at Reading Rugby Club, play in international competitions and follow Saracens, really tells them something about your physical attributes, team skills and enthusiasm.

Top tips on writing your CV
- Don't be modest – sell yourself.
- Include anything that shows that you are a dependable, responsible, reliable person.
- Direct it to fit the job you are applying for.
- Each section should be in chronological order with most recent events first.
- Remember the finished version should generally not be longer than two sides of A4.
- Keep re-drafting it until you get it right.
- Always revise and update your CV when applying for a new job.

Chapter 2
Personal Details

The first section of the CV should not present any problems! This simply includes basic information and contact details about yourself so that an employer can reach you should they wish you to come for an interview, for example. There are no tricks here, just make sure you include any contact information that will be useful.

You don't have to include all of the items listed below, but since applications will vary, I have commented on all these headings:

Personal details
- Name
- Address
- Post code
- Daytime telephone
- Evening telephone
- Fax
- Mobile telephone
- E-mail

- Date of birth
- Sex
- Marital status
- Children
- Nationality
- Driving licence and car ownership
- Non-smoker
- Photograph

Name and address

Show your full name as the heading for your CV – we will look at presentation in Chapter 11.

Give your full contact address including the correct postcode.

Telephone, fax and e-mail

List both daytime and evening telephone numbers if you can, including the area codes. If you do not want to be telephoned at work, then do not give the number at this stage, but make sure that you have a messaging service on your phone at home. If you don't have an answerphone, it is free for BT customers to subscribe to their service. Make sure your voicemail message, if you have one, is clear and business-like and presents a professional image. Get rid of any cute or funny responses. The company may phone to arrange an interview or to ask for more information and your voice message will add to the picture they are forming of you – and you can't rely on the fact that they will share your sense of humour! Don't forget to check your messages regularly.

Give a fax number if you have one. This can be useful to confirm an interview date or send additional information, although don't worry if you don't have one as it is not often used.

Giving your mobile phone number obviously means you will be accessible at any time convenient to the company. This is extremely useful in making arrangements for an interview or to answer additional questions an employer may have about your CV, before they decide whether or not they will interview you. It is worth putting the company number into your phone book so that you recognise who is calling you before you answer the phone. You can then make sure you answer in a business-like way and don't mistake them for a mate and say something you'd regret! Again, check that your voicemail message is appropriate.

All firms now use e-mail as a quick and efficient means of communication, so it is an advantage if you can give an e-mail contact address. If you are not online at home, set up a webmail account such as Hotmail and make sure you are able to access it regularly at a friend's house, at work or at an internet café. Use a sensible e-mail address and one that is easily recognisable and not easy to mis-key.

Other information

You will often see these last sections on example CVs, so it is important to think about whether they may be relevant to your application and therefore whether you wish to include them. None of them is obligatory on a CV, and none of them should be a determining factor in whether or not you get a job, so it is not compulsory to include them.

For example, it is not essential to give your date of birth, and increasingly this question is considered ageist and discriminatory to the more mature applicant. If it is important to the employer they will ask you about it at the interview or on the application form. It is rarely necessary to include your gender, marital status or whether or not you have a family.

There may be some circumstances, however, in which one of these pieces of information may be relevant, and it will show that you have thought about your application if you supply that information from the outset. For example, if you are applying for a job as a sales representative, the company will need to know that you can drive and, hopefully, have a full, clean driving licence. Your age may also be important from an insurance point of view. If the job you are applying for may involve travelling abroad, your nationality and passport details could be relevant to the company. If the company's offices are in the countryside without a regular bus or train service, it is reassuring to a prospective employer to know that you can get to work reliably.

As most companies have policies relating to smoking in the workplace, it can be helpful to state that you are a non-smoker on your CV. If you do smoke, do not comment, but be prepared to be asked about it at the interview. Make sure that you give the interviewer an assurance that you will conform to any company rules relating to smoking at work.

Don't send photographs unless they are specifically asked for. This is rarely a requirement at the CV stage. You may, however, be required to provide photos for a security pass if you are made a job offer.

Top tips on personal details
- Don't include irrelevant personal information such as your marital status unless it has direct relevance to your ability to do the job.
- Make sure you have a sensible e-mail address, not the fun one you use on MSN.
- Ensure you have a professional answerphone or voicemail message set up.

Chapter 3
Personal Profile

This comprises a concise description of who you are, what you have achieved to date and what you hope to achieve, and is your first opportunity to capture the reader's attention and give a possible employer a picture of you as a person and a competent employee. When the prospective employer reads your CV they are looking for the answer to two questions. Does this person have the right experience, knowledge, skill and attitude to do the job? Are they worth inviting for an interview?

Your personal profile should describe you in the workplace and comment on your personal qualities, competence, knowledge, experience and relevant skills. Think about what you would like an employer to know about you if you only had 100 words or so in which to sell yourself. Invest time and effort in this section, as it is the first section the employer will read so it is essential that it captures their imagination or sparks their interest enough to make them read on.

Although this snapshot should come early in your CV once it is finished, it is actually a good idea to jot down notes in this section while you are compiling the rest of the document, then return to it at the end. By that time, you will have thought a lot about what matters most to you and to your potential employer, which will make this resumé easier to write.

It is usual to write this section in the third person, although you can use the first person if you feel it is more appropriate to the job you are applying for.

Remember to keep focused on the positive. Do not include any information that could be construed as a negative or that has no bearing on whether you can do the job.

It is not vitally important to include a personal profile or career aim in a CV. They are especially irrelevant if you include one and make unsubstantiated statements. Before including this section, think carefully; ask yourself whether the information you wish to include would be better suited to being written into your covering letter, where you will have more room to develop your text and state evidence to support your claims. If you do decide to include this section, it is imperative that you keep your statements specific and include facts which can be backed up with evidence.

Personal profile
- Brief character description
- Career profile
- Career objectives
- Key skills

Brief character description and career profile

This is the most concise description you can give of the point you have reached in your career. If you are just starting out and looking for a first job, then obviously this will not be necessary, although you could look briefly at what you feel you have achieved educationally to date.

It is a common problem that we all tend to undervalue what we can offer, so start by thinking positive – it will pay off. We all have something special to offer, whether it is personal qualities, a skill or knowledge. Just think positive about what you have to offer, and make sure that the words that you use are descriptive and promote your abilities and positive qualities.

Begin with a list of words and phrases that you feel you could work into your description. Ask yourself some questions to help you focus and use the answers as a starting point on which to build your profile.

● What are the positive things you would say about yourself?
● What are the good things that a friend would say about you?
● What would your head teacher or tutor say about you?
● What did your last appraisal say about you?
● What did your last boss say about you?

While you are working on your profile, remember that you will be applying for a specific job and you will need to use words and phrases relevant to the job you are applying for. There's a lot more detail on this in Chapter 10 (see page 60).

Positive language

Use this list of positive, descriptive words to get some ideas. You can use them to create your statement or use words of your own which you feel more closely reflect the real you. It is not a complete list, but should help to get you thinking along the right lines.

Ability and commitment to tackle problems and achieve a solution	Ability to motivate and manage
	Able
	Able to cope under pressure
Ability to communicate with all levels	Able to focus on
	Accurate
Ability to get results	Achievement in

Personal Profile

Acquired a comprehensive range
  of
Adaptable
All aspects of
Ambitious
An excellent track record
Analytical
Application
Articulate
Assertive
Assist
Background in
Capable
Careful
Committed
Competent
Confident
Considerable
  experience/knowledge
Co-operative
Creative
Dedicated
Deliver
Dependable
Dynamic
Eager to prove myself
Effective
Efficient

Energetic
Enjoy a challenge and finding
  appropriate solutions
Enthusiastic
Excellent organisational/
  interpersonal/administrative
  skills
Experienced
Flexible
Fluent in
Follows through
Good communication
  written/verbal skills
Good humoured
Good working knowledge of
Gregarious
Hardworking
Innovative
Keen interest in
Keen to learn
Liaise
Looking for an opportunity to
  make a contribution/to use/ to
  demonstrate
Looking for an opportunity to
  prove
Meet deadlines
Motivated

23

Multilingual/Bilingual
Negotiation
Open-minded
Organised
Pays attention to detail
People-orientated
Persevere
Practical
Proactive
Problem-solving skills
Professional
Profit-orientated/driven
Qualified
Quick to learn
Receptive to change/new ideas
Reliable
Resourceful
Responsible
Self-motivated
Self-reliant
Skill developed through
  experience
Skilled
Specific experience of
Successful

Tactful
Thorough
Thorough understanding of
Thorough working knowledge of
Trained
Trustworthy
Valuable experience
Versatile
Willing
Willing to learn
With a detailed knowledge of
With a highly developed
  responsible approach
With a solid foundation in
With an excellent track record in
With an up-to-date working
  knowledge of
With proven skills
With sound technical background
  in
With specific expertise in
With specific interest in
With wide experience of
Works well within a team
Works well under pressure

Once you have a collection of descriptive words, then work them into a statement that encapsulates your personality and attitude. You don't have a lot of space on a CV, so try to focus on information that would not otherwise be included in the document. Use your present or previous job title to describe yourself – 'an experienced clerical assistant' – as it immediately gives the reader useful information about what you are able to do. Keep it positive, and leave out anything which could sound like 'I am desperate for work and will take any job'. Leave out negative irrelevant personal details and concentrate on what you have to offer in relation to the job you are applying for.

Examples of career profiles

Here are some examples to get you started. They are not intended to show the whole scope of an applicant's experience and capabilities but to give a concise introductory snapshot. I have related them to specific job requirements so you can see how to tailor your profile to your chosen career. In the case of a speculative application, use the words and phrases that fit best with the work you would like to do.

The employer wants

A driver with a clean HGV driving licence who must have experience in delivering to trade and private customers. Ability to assist in planning his or her own delivery schedule an advantage. The successful applicant will be required to resolve customer queries at the point of delivery and liaise with head office stores supplies department.

Personal profile

An experienced delivery driver holding a clean HGV licence, with ten years' experience of delivering spare parts in the Home Counties. Experienced in delivering to trade and private customers, organising and planning own workload. Equally competent in resolving customer queries at the door, or liaising with HO departments.

The employer wants
An administrator. Applicants should be highly organised, dependable, able to work independently or as part of a team, with experience in dealing with telephone queries and responding to correspondence.

Personal profile
A competent administrator with excellent written and verbal skills who is seeking a position which offers the opportunity to put them into practice. A quick learner, hard working and trustworthy, who remains good tempered under pressure and is used to prioritising a demanding workload.

The employer wants
A private secretary. A highly organised and trustworthy private secretary for our Human Resources Manager. The successful applicant will be required to provide full secretarial support and will have excellent keyboard skills, good interpersonal skills and the ability to function at all levels, including Board level.

Personal profile
A highly organised and discreet private secretary able to provide competent secretarial support. Experienced in dealing with all correspondence, from typing confidential reports and taking minutes up to and including Board level. Loyal and supportive with well-developed interpersonal skills, used to using own initiative and prioritising a demanding workload.

The employer wants
A customer service adviser. The successful applicant will be expected to assist with customer service issues and administrative duties in our busy service department. A knowledge of Excel is a must. You will have the ability to work under pressure and respond to a variety of enquiries, whilst remaining calm and helpful when dealing with our clients.

Personal profile
An experienced customer services adviser with excellent communication skills and administrative skills, proficient with both manual and computerised systems, with specific knowledge of Excel. Experienced in conflict management and in dealing with a variety of service issues. Enjoys a challenge. Able to work under pressure and remain good humoured, calm and helpful at all times.

The employer wants
An accounts assistant. To be successful in this role you will be highly numerate, with a proven background in accounts procedures. You will be required to manage your own workload and work as part of the accounts team, assisting with a variety of procedures on request.

Personal profile
A competent, highly numerate accounts assistant, experienced in a variety of accounting office procedures including purchase and bought ledgers and in assisting in the preparation of end-of-year accounts. An individual who is co-operative and efficient, able to work effectively independently or as a team member.

The employer wants
An experienced manager to oversee their busy town-centre fast-food restaurant. The successful applicant must have a solid background in catering and catering management and demonstrable commitment to achieving results whilst maintaining standards. They will be required to set targets, and manage and motivate staff.

Personal profile
A professional catering manager experienced in catering and management techniques gained while with a major restaurant chain. Proven skills in the training and motivation of staff resulting in demonstrable improved customer services standards, with a track record of achievement and abilities in setting targets and achieving goals.

Career objectives

This section is where you can touch on your basic career ambitions. Do you have a specific career aim? Are you making a speculative application to an employer with a view to entering a particular industry? Is this the ultimate job for you, or a way of gaining experience and knowledge on the way towards something else? Here you have a chance to make a statement about the sort of position you are looking for.

A career aim or objective is a short statement about what you hope to achieve by this application. It tells the employer what you are aiming for. It is particularly useful if you are making a speculative approach to a company as it will give them an idea of what type of position you are looking for. If you are responding to a specific advertisement, make sure that your career objective fits the opportunities offered by the prospective employer and outlined in the advertisement. Remember that it is not an essay, just a short concise statement of a few sentences. If you wish, you can make it part of your career profile.

While it would be unwise to suggest that you see any job as a stop-gap, don't be afraid to show your ambition to learn and to progress. If you are starting out on your career, any employer who is worth working for should be able to spot and hopefully direct your ambition for his or her benefit and yours. If you are applying for a job that you know will give you valuable experience over, say, a two-year period, after which you may want to move on, simply present this with the most positive spin.

Examples of career objectives

These examples should give you some ideas on what to put in your statement and show how you can combine the personal career profile with aims and objectives.

Example one

A dynamic, highly motivated sales professional with over ten years' experience selling to the civil engineering and construction industry is seeking the opportunity to move into general management in a major construction company. Has a thorough understanding of construction methods, drawings and plans. Equally at home on site or in the Board room. Excellent communication and interpersonal skills with the ability to work to deadlines and get results.

Example two

A hardworking and self-motivated graduate with well-developed problem-solving and analytical skills, who enjoys meeting new challenges and seeing them through to completion, is looking for a position within a progressive research department with the opportunity to contribute to the development of the company's products, growth and prosperity.

Example three

A reliable individual, capable and quick to learn and with a commitment to customer service, is now seeking an opportunity with more responsibility within the retail industry to develop service and managerial skills.

Example four

A conscientious and responsible school leaver, with a good school record. An individual who is keen to learn and can be relied upon to do their best, is looking for a position which offers opportunities for training and development, including the opportunity to join an apprenticeship scheme.

Top tips on career profiles and objectives
- Keep it concise and targeted on your personal skills and experience in the workplace to set the tone for the rest of the CV.
- Keep it relevant to the job you are applying for.
- Be prepared to discuss or explain your statement at an interview.

Key skills

This section is about the skills you have acquired to date and is another opportunity to attract the reader's attention and hold their interest. It should not be a list of what you can do, but an illustration of your primary skills to indicate in which area of work you are most effective. For example, some people are brilliant organisers, good with detail, forward planning and structure. Other people tend to be carers with highly developed people skills. You may have an outgoing personality and enjoy being hands-on, or more introspective and happier working with a computer screen. Don't try to give the impression that you have the type of personality you think the employer is looking for if it is not accurate – even if you did manage to fool the employer at interview, it wouldn't be the right job for you.

Use this section to highlight your experience, knowledge, career achievements, training, academic achievements and key skills, whether practical, manual or managerial. Comment on successes in your working life and highlight the main skills or knowledge you have to offer, particularly those relevant to the job you are applying for. Mention successful management decisions, management strategies implemented and special projects completed. Stress management responsibilities and job-related skills. Specifically comment on IT skills and include knowledge of relevant software packages.

You should include training undertaken and successfully completed and a brief synopsis of the course content and experience gained. If you did not finish a training course, you can still include it, but be prepared to answer questions on why you dropped out or did not complete it. Some employers may require you to complete the course or qualification as a condition of the job offer, and in these circumstances may offer to fund it or offer you day release to complete the course if they feel it would enable you to do the job more effectively. Make sure you tell the interviewer that you are keen to take advantage of an opportunity to complete the course, if that is what the company requires.

Remember to include things that may seem obvious to you: keyboard and computer skills, people-management and supervisory skills, knowledge of procedures, the ability to operate types of machinery or procedures and policies.

Include experience or skills gained thorough voluntary work, schemes such as the Prince's Trust, part-time or temporary work. Mention ways you have 'grown' in maturity, confidence or understanding. Include any contributions to trade-based publications.

Positive language
Look at this list of positive words (and the one on pages 22–24) to give you ideas regarding the language to use in your statement. Make sure that you use the most appropriate words to tell a prospective employer something about what you have done and what you can do.

Accessed	Assisted	Consistent
Achieved	Balanced	Constructed
Acquired	Budgeted	Constructive
Adaptable	Commissioned	Consulted
Adviser	Committed	Contemporary
Ambitious	Communicative	Contributed
Analysed	Competitive	Controlled
Appointed	Conceived	Conviction
Arranged	Conscientious	Co-ordinating

Correlated
Created
Defined
Determined
Discipline
Discussed
Experienced in
devising and
implementing
Extensive contacts
Flair
Formulated
Founded
Gained an
understanding of

Handled
Headed
Helped
Instructing
Knowledge of
Maintaining
Managing people/
systems /processes
Perceptive
Persistent
Personable
Persuasive
Pertinent
Planning and
implementing

Presentation skills
Proficiency
Running research
projects
Set up
Skilled
Successfully
Support
Tactful
Taught
Thorough
Understand
Winning
Writing detailed
reports

Examples of key skills

These examples should help you draw up your own statement.

Example one

The applicant has the following key skills:

- Successfully completed the HandS training course and was appointed Health and Safety Officer for the Lipsons group.
- Revised and updated the Company Health and Safety manual on procedures used by the six stores of the group.
- Devised and delivered staff training for all grades on HandS practices.
- Successfully introduced a No Smoking policy.
- Gained an understanding of the problems of tobacco addiction.

Example two
The applicant has the following key skills:
- Six years' experience supervising the night shift on a major car production line.
- Responsible for maintaining company quality control standards.
- A thorough understanding of BS quality control standards.
- Consistently achieved production targets.
- Dealt with disciplinary issues as necessary.

Example three
The applicant has the following key skills:
- The ability to get results through the management and motivation of the sales team.
- Achieved the prestigious Top Team award for three consecutive years.
- Increased sales by 15 per cent annually year on year.
- Successfully completed the Diploma in Marketing course.
- Devised and delivered training seminars for sales personnel.
- Contributed an article on direct selling to *Sales Talk* magazine.

Example four
The applicant has the following key skills:
- Excellent keyboard skills.
- A helpful and efficient telephone manner.
- Considerable experience of busy switchboards.
- A thorough understanding of paging and messaging systems.

Example five

The applicant has the following key skills:

- Increased the financial performance of the group by 5 per cent.
- Successfully developed and implemented the strategy for trade initiatives in Far Eastern countries.
- Reduced and rationalised operating costs within the group through improved quality control methods.
- Introduced a staff profit-sharing scheme based on results.
- Co-ordinated and managed change successfully throughout the three companies of the group.
- Successfully completed a public speaking on television course.

Top tips on key skills

- Tell a prospective employer what you can do in a concise professional statement, highlighting the elements pertinent to the job.
- Match your statement to the employer's requirements.
- If it's your first job, highlight any work experience and special responsibilities at school, college or university.

Chapter 4

Education and Training

A history of your schooling is not required here, but simply the details of your educational qualifications and any professional qualifications you may hold. As usual, start with the most recent. Don't omit details such as your A level grades or dates as the prospective employer will probably think the worst.

If this is your first CV after leaving full-time education you will want to place this section before your work experience. If you are an applicant who completed further education then the more closely related your qualifications are to the job, the more details you should include. All degree courses, for example, encourage analytical thinking, problem-solving and a logical approach to learning. Many also develop practical or communication skills. No two courses will be completely alike, and you want to ensure that the employer is clear about what you have studied, and not follow his or her own preconceptions about what that particular course might involve. If you are writing your CV about five years after leaving education and you have been or are employed, then it will be your employment record which is more likely to capture the reader's attention initially. As a result, this section would therefore come before your education section.

If you are an applicant who did not achieve academic success, place more emphasis on your work record, including temporary jobs or work experience, to show the prospective employer that you have work-related skills, knowledge and experience. Concentrate on any training you have received and your employment record as this will be a far more accurate measure of your skills and abilities than the number of GCSEs you can offer.

It is usual to start with your most recent achievements first:

Education and training
- Professional qualifications and training
- Membership of relevant professional bodies
- University or higher or further education establishments
- Dates
- Qualifications and achievements
- School/College
- Dates
- Qualifications and achievements

Professional qualifications and memberships

If you have a higher degree, such as a Master's, or professional qualifications, list the details here first. Give the university or professional organisation responsible for the qualification and the date it was awarded.

Also include any memberships of professional bodies, as these indicate the quality of your application. If you have received any academic prizes or have had your academic work published, it may be useful to include information about it here.

You can also list specific work-related training courses, including short courses on management topics, occupational training courses or courses to gain a craft or computer skill, or knowledge of specific software packages. Include involvement in re-training or job creation, or special schemes such as the Prince's Trust. Include details of diplomas or certificates awarded.

Higher or further education

You do not need to give full addresses, but simply the name of the university or college and the town. List the dates of attendance in years only; employers will know that they will follow the academic year.

Indicate the qualification you hold and the level of achievement; for example, BA (Hons) English Language and Literature (upper second class).

Include any additional qualifications or achievements that are most appropriate in this section of the form, such as positions of responsibility.

Schools

Again, simply include the school or college name and town, with the year-dates you attended.

List the subjects and the grades you attained at A level, or similar qualifications such as BTEC. Include any special distinctions, if relevant. You should list your GCSE subjects but you do not need to show your grades on your CV, although you should be prepared to give details at the interview if necessary.

If you are older with a long work history, you may simply wish to list the number and level of your educational qualifications: 3 A Levels; 10 O Levels. (Information for younger readers: O Levels and CSEs were the two qualifications combined to create GCSEs.)

If you are a recent school leaver, the employer will focus on your school record, so include details of achievements such as NVQs, Duke of Edinburgh Award Schemes, Prefect, Team Captain, Head of House, and so on.

Examples of education and training

Example one

2001–2005	University of Bangor
	PhD Clinical Psychology
Subjects covered:	Clinical Psychology
	Cognitive Neuroscience
	Language, Learning and Development
Publications:	Dementia Services in the UK
	Modern Psychology, Hober & Hober, 2002

Example two

2002–2005	University of East Anglia
	BA (Hons) History 2:2 (expected)
Modules:	The Renaissance
	World Wars I and II
	Industrial Revolution
	Mussolini, Stalin and Hitler

Education and Training ——————————————————————

| Final Year | |
| Dissertation: | The Impact of the New World |

1995–2001	Woodcroft School
	A Levels: English (A), History (A), Art (A)
	AS Levels: French (B)
	GCSEs: Eight subjects including
	Mathematics and English (2 A*s, 3 As, 3 Bs)

Responsibilities: Prefect and Air Cadet.

Other achievements: Certificate of competence in Information
Technology (Distinction), including
spreadsheets, word processing and desk-top
publishing.
Knowledge of Word, Access and Excel.

Example three
1996–2002   Rochester High School
GCSEs: Maths, English, Double Science,
History, Art, Spanish

Other achievements: Elected team captain for two years for the
school's under-15's football team.
Hosted visiting teams.

Providing proof

It is not unusual to be asked to prove your attainments by showing your certificates, and this will certainly be the case if you apply to government departments or district councils, hospitals, and so on. Keep your certificates safely with all your CV information and letters of application so that you are ready to supply them when required. It might be useful to have a couple of copies taken, but generally employers will expect to see the original document.

Top tips on education
- List your history in chronological order with the most recent first.
- Place more emphasis on your higher qualifications or recent training.
- Don't list your school qualifications and achievements in too much detail, just give basic facts and highlight special achievements.
- Remember to include team captaincy or similar roles that show leadership qualities.
- Use bullet points to highlight your responsibilities and achievements and to draw attention to your abilities and capabilities.

Chapter 5
Career History

This section tells a prospective employer which companies you have worked for, whether as a permanent, part-time, temporary or voluntary worker, how long you were there, and what you did there, so you need to give specific information on the company names, the dates you worked there, your job title, a brief description of what you did for them and what you achieved. In other words, include a short explanation of your duties, responsibilities and capabilities. List any successes and achievements, in particular those which have a direct bearing on the requirements of the job you are applying for.

Career history
- Job title
- Company name and address
- Dates of employment
- Responsibilities
- Key experience
- Key achievements
- Skills gained

Job title

For each job, give your accurate job title. If the new employer does eventually follow up your references, they would soon find out if you had given yourself a promotion!

Company name and address

Give the full company name. If relevant, you may want to include the town in which it is situated, but you don't need the complete address. If the firm is in a large city, you may want to give 'London SE1', for example. If you get to an interview, the possible employer may want the full address and dates relevant to your job history, so have them available if necessary.

If the type of business is not clear from the company name, it may be worth including that in brackets; for example, M.C. Clarke and Co. Ltd (Central-heating engineers).

Dates of employment

Start with your most recent employer and work backwards from there. A month and year are perfectly adequate for your starting and leaving dates in each case, although you can simply give the year if the jobs were some time ago. What the employer wants to see is that you have the staying power to remain in a job for a reasonable length of time, and perhaps also the ambition to progress at a reasonable rate.

It is usual to show about ten years' work history, but you can include earlier employment if it will be beneficial and is pertinent to your application. In the event of an application for the public service sector or a position involving working with children, going into people's homes, the police force or hospital service, an employer may request details of your employment history for a period longer than ten years. They will normally have a statement to that effect on the application form or in the content of the job advertisement. In any event if you feel that it would be helpful or relevant to your application, you can include earlier experience.

If you believe that it would be an advantage to provide information for a longer period, then either do so in a short statement or incorporate it into your covering letter or CV. For example: Prior to joining Smith & Co. I served for 12 years in HRH Royal Engineers, both at home and abroad, and gained a thorough understanding of bridge construction methods.

At this stage you do not have to include reasons for leaving the various jobs unless this puts a positive spin on your career history. For example, if you were head-hunted or singled out for promotion, you might want to include that. When you come to interview, however, the interviewer is likely to ask you why you changed jobs, and especially why you are looking for a change now, as this information is important to the interviewer in building up a picture of who you are and what motivates you.

Responsibilities, key experience, key achievements and skills gained

You may want to treat these sections separately to begin with, then combine them into a short descriptive paragraph or bulleted points. That helps you to focus on the different areas of your job.

Include any temporary work you have done, particularly if you have been unemployed for a long period or you are straight out of school or university. It shows that you have the work ethic and that you have followed procedures and carried out tasks to an established standard. You would also have gained knowledge and learned skills even if the work was fairly mundane.

Don't leave career gaps unanswered. British employers like to be able to track your employment record fully. If you spent a period travelling, include it; it shows that you have experience of dealing with different situations and people, and is viewed by most employers in a very positive light. For other gaps in your employment record, explain them as briefly as possible and be prepared to give the specific dates of your employment record and fuller details at an interview.

Experience is a valuable commodity to an employer and if you are quite a way down your career path, or if your educational achievements are not too impressive, focus your CV on your employment record, and the skills, knowledge and experience you have gained, as this will be far more important to a prospective employer at that stage in your career.

Provide a brief description of what you did in the job, your duties and responsibilities and the skills, knowledge or experience you gained so that the employer can see the scope of the work you have been used to, how you relate in a team situation, whether you have leadership skills, if you can work under pressure, and if you are prepared to do mundane jobs as part of your role if necessary. You could refer to management skills, craft skills or any other personal abilities. Remember to emphasise information specific to the job you are applying for. Treat time spent in the Armed Forces in the same way as a civilian job history and show progress, responsibilities and achievements in descending order with the highest and best first. For more senior positions, you will obviously require more detail regarding the areas of skill and responsibility in your job.

Examples of responsibilities, key experience, key achievements and skills gained

Example one
Supervised a team of four people dealing with customers and suppliers to ensure quality control across the range of products; undertook all office administration tasks; dealt with customers and suppliers by letter and telephone; maintained a full information database; ensured schedules were maintained and was responsible for problem solving.

Example two
Retail assistant involved in all departments of a major store; dealt with customers; managed incoming deliveries; supervised product displays; responsible for accuracy and security of finances in each department.

Example three
Followed designated procedures to check quality, safety and production standards of children's toys and pack them safely and securely.

Example four
Cleaner for a large restaurant. Acquired an understanding of the various cleaning chemicals and how to use them to best effect on different surfaces.

Example five
Used to working as a team and to tight deadlines, maintaining accuracy in data input and evaluation.

Give facts and figures in your descriptions of your capabilities wherever possible, to support your claims. Employers want people who can do the job well and fit in with their organisation. Your CV, therefore, should convince them that you can do just that. Focus the information on your highest skill levels and most recent employment.

Examples of career history

Example one
Wendham Books
1998–2004   Sales Executive
                     Sales Manager
- Optimised sales opportunities through improved product knowledge training for sales team, achieving a 20 per cent increase in sales turnover.
- Introduced an improved customer aftercare package, achieving a drop of 10 per cent in customer complaints.
- Motivated, managed and trained sales staff.
- Responsible for setting sales targets and allocating territories for 7 sales personnel.
- Conducted an analysis of sales results linked to gross margins.
- Achieved the Top Salesman 1999 award.
- Promoted to Sales Manager 2001.

Example two
Book Mart, London EC2
1994–1998   Sales Executive
                      Trainee Sales Representative
- Responsible for the development of the mail order business.
- Consistently met and exceeded sales targets.
- Expanded sales in the Maidstone area, achieving a 30 per cent increase in sales volume.

Read-it book wholesalers, Nottingham
1990–1994   Warehouse Assistant
- Responsible for correct storage and cataloguing of the book stock.
- Participated in sales promotional events.
- Undertook and completed the Tack correspondence course in selling techniques.

Top tips on career history
- Start with your most recent employment and work backwards.
- Cover, approximately, the last ten years.
- Don't leave career gaps unanswered.
- Don't use jargon or abbreviations unless they are universally known and understood.
- Include facts and figures to support your statements if necessary.
- Be prepared to give additional information at an interview.

Chapter 6

Special Skills and Abilities

This is a chance to include any additional skills that don't fall into any other categories. For some people, this section may not be relevant as their skills will either be directly work-related or apply to their academic career, so may have been included elsewhere. However, for people who have followed a less direct career path or perhaps have a very broad skills base, this can be an important way of showing their qualities and strengths.

By definition, it is impossible to give a comprehensive list of headings for this section, but if it applies to you, the following ideas will give you useful guidelines so that you can develop your own CV information.

Special skills and abilities
- Positions of responsibility
- Special training or skills
- Achievements
- Language skills
- Publications
- Testimonials

Positions of responsibility

If you have not already included these in your educational section, list any special responsibilities you have undertaken.

Special training or skills

This may include first aid qualifications, health and safety training, or perhaps the ability to use sign language. It could also cover specialist computer skills.

Achievements

Perhaps you have organised a major charity event, led a mountain-climbing expedition or had an art exhibition in your local civic hall. If it is relevant to your application, then consider including it in this section.

Language skills

Language skills can be an important asset in a global market, so do let your employer know your level of competence in written or spoken languages.

Publications

If you have published articles, or even books, or been a magazine editor or have other similar achievements, they should be included.

Testimonials

If an employer or teacher has given you a particularly strong testimonial, you may wish to quote some of it here, with a note of the qualifications of the source, for example, 'my last appraisal rated me a "highly competent manager"'.

Chapter 7

Interests and Activities

It is obvious why an employer wants to know about your education and career history, but it is important when you are completing this section to keep focused on why they want to know more about your personal interests. This section is designed to tell them more about you as a person so that they can see how you are likely to approach the job and how you will fit in as a member of the team. It can also help them find out if your out-of-office activities could cause a problem to your attendance record or health and well-being.

Don't claim to be interested in something you know little about just to impress. Interviewers often ask about your interests at interviews to relax you, so if you include reading, expect to be asked who your favourite authors are and why, or what you are reading at the moment.

Keep your comments in this section brief and accurate, and be ready to talk more about them at the interview.

Interests and activities
- Reading, research, computers
- Outdoor activities, such as hiking or biking
- Craft skills, such as painting or repairing electrical equipment
- Sports activities and team membership
- Musical interests and abilities

Chapter 8
References

The people you give as referees should be responsible and trustworthy people who will give an honest – and hopefully complimentary – opinion about you to an employer. Ideally, their picture of you should match the one you have given of yourself – another reason to keep your CV accurate and not to exaggerate.

You don't have to give names or details on your CV at this stage but you should indicate that they are 'available on request'. If you know you are in the process of job-hunting and will need to call on your referees in due course, however, it makes sense to speak in advance with the people you would like to act as referees so that you can supply their details immediately on request. This is especially important if you are attending an interview, as you could be asked for this information at the end of the interview or if you are required to fill in the company application form. Always ask the person for permission first, before you give their name, to see if they are prepared to give you a reference and if it is acceptable for a prospective employer to contact them. It is helpful to inform your referees of what you are currently doing, your applications, activities and aspirations. It will aid them in writing a pertinent reference.

References
- Name and title (Mr, Dr, Prof, etc.)
- Address
- Telephone
- E-mail
- Job title and/or an indication of how they know you
- How long they have known you

Name and title

Who should you choose? One referee should be your current or last employer. If this is a problem for any reason – perhaps you don't want them to know you are applying for other jobs – you should expect your prospective employer to ask why and be prepared to give an honest and logical answer. You should ask someone who has worked directly with you who can give an accurate judgement on your capabilities. Your second referee should be someone who knows you well, but preferably in a work environment. Try to choose a second referee who is not going to repeat what the first may say.

If you are leaving school or university, you can ask a personal tutor, departmental professor or lecturer, or perhaps the careers adviser. Avoid relatives, heads or teachers from school, if you are not a school/university leaver, as it may look as though you have made no impact since that time.

If you have not worked for sometime or are re-entering the job market after a break, try and find someone in a responsible position who can vouch for your professional qualities. It is always better to choose a business contact rather than a friend, although if you do choose a friend, it is best to ask someone you have known for some time and who the prospective employer can recognise as being in a position to give an unbiased reference.

Address, telephone and e-mail

Find out whether you should use the person's home or office address and which telephone number and/or e-mail address is convenient. If they would prefer to be contacted by one or other method, then include this information for your prospective employer.

Job title and/or an indication of how they know you

If your referee has a specific job title or professional qualifications, include these with your information to emphasise their reliability and trustworthy nature.

You should state how the referee knows you and how long they have known you, again so that your prospective employer can judge the reliability of the reference.

Open testimonials

If you know you are going to take a break from employment before applying for another job, or you have not found a new job before you leave your present company, it is quite acceptable to ask for a reference to take with you, although not all companies will be prepared to do this.

Additional reference information

If you have just left full-time education, then your results and school reports or UCAS profile could be of interest to the prospective employer.

Chapter 9

What if You Don't Fit the Mould?

There are some applicants for whom the task of creating a CV does not flow as smoothly because, for one reason or another, their educational or career history is slightly out of the ordinary. This need not be a problem. Keep in mind the purpose of the CV: to give an employer an accurate and positive indication of your skills and abilities. Think through the various headings most usually used for a CV and make your notes. Then start to think beyond convention.

● What else puts me in a good light that has not been mentioned?
● Should I re-order the sections?
● Where should the most positive focus be?
● Would it be better to use concise text rather than bullet points?

Poor academic record

If you know this section of your CV is weak in relation to the job you are applying for, then it is up to you to compensate by stressing your strengths in other areas. It is more likely that you will have an opportunity to discuss this at an interview, but if you feel that your CV will be rejected for this reason beforehand, it may be worth considering a brief comment, perhaps in your covering letter, to direct the prospective employer's attention to your subsequent work record.

Mature students

Experience, maturity and broad-ranging skills in different areas are just some of the advantages mature students can offer an employer so you need to promote these advantages. People who have taken a degree later in life will need to explain why they have made the choice to go back to studying, and how their knowledge, experience and outlook have changed. You will have no problems in putting this in a positive light for an employer.

Career changes

If you have had a lot of different jobs, you need to explain why and how you benefited from that variety, to show an employer that you are able to focus and not just flit from one job to another at random. Turn your experience into a positive by emphasising what you have learnt from the variety and showing why you have now made the choice of job for which you are applying. Give concrete reasons to show that you now have a more mature approach and intend to remain in the new position for a reasonable length of time.

If you have made (or are making) a single, major career change, it is a good idea to indicate why you have chosen to do so, and the benefits you can offer from both career tracks.

If you have had a gap in your career, explain briefly why and how you benefited from it.

Childcare break

If you have had a break in order to raise a family, don't fall into the stereotype of under-rating the qualities that are required for this 'job'. It may not be paid but it is a highly complex, responsible and rewarding one. Think about it in professional terms and use appropriate language and key-skills designations to describe it. You can then help to break down a resistance that does exist among some employers by looking at this time realistically.

Think about the skills that are required: responsibility, commitment, multi-tasking, communication, caring, teaching – and there are many more.

Don't forget to include voluntary work you have done during this time. Perhaps you have been a part of the PTA or a self-help group committee member, helped to support teachers in lesson or craft activities, or taken on other roles.

Circumstances where you may fear prejudice

If you fear there may be aspects of your life which might encourage an employer to discriminate against you, it is worth thinking how best to approach this within your job application. At some point it is likely you will have to raise the issue and to a degree the timing of this can be down to you. It could be worthwhile disclosing the evidence early on in your job application by stating it in your covering letter or CV, as an employer may welcome your honesty and perceive you as mature and trustworthy. It is understandable, however, if you feel that disclosing any such circumstances early on might hinder your chances of being offered an interview.

If you do decide to omit information such as disability or long periods of unemployment, be prepared to answer questions regarding this at the interview.

The following are situations where discrimination can occur, with tips on how to convey such circumstances as positively as possible in a CV.

Unemployment or a significant career break

If you have had a long period of unemployment or are you re-entering the job market after a significant break, then you will be asked about this. Make sure you show the positive use you have made of your time – skills learned, initiatives taken or courses followed – and the efforts you have made to gain employment.

You may be out of date on some things and lot could have changed since you were last employed, but some things don't. Prospective employers will still be looking for good, reliable, able employees who are keen to prove themselves. And a lot of your skills will still be relevant. For instance, your interpersonal skills and communication skills will be valued, and you may have honed your computer skills through increased use of your home computer.

If you haven't already done so, why not take full advantage of the various retraining schemes on offer and enrol on one? It could be helpful for updating your skills, or may introduce you to a whole new career opportunity. You can do it whilst you continue with your job search. The retraining programmes will get you back into the work ethic, and make you familiar with the work-place jargon again, in addition to updating or learning a new skill.

Don't tell prospective employers what you haven't done – I have been out of work for five years … I have no skills or training, as I have been at home looking after the family for the last 20 years … I am over 50 … I have had a lot of jobs and very little experience – emphasise the positive. Concentrate on the life skills and experience you have acquired during your period out of work, or your achievement in learning a new skill through retraining.

Criminal record

You should check the status of any conviction; it may not be necessary to mention it in a CV or at an interview. If it is relevant, you may be better to mention it briefly and in the most positive light in a covering letter. It is not a good idea to try to hide relevant convictions that could be discovered at a later date; this will not convey the positive impression you want to give the employer.

Health problems or disabilities

There is no reason to mention anything that has no bearing on your ability to do the job in question. If it is likely to affect your ability to do the job, then it is in your interests to mention the issue and explain how you cope with any problems that arise, and the best place for this is probably the covering letter you send with your CV. If you are likely to have to undergo a medical examination for a job, then you should mention anything that will emerge at that time.

Top tips on thinking outside the box
- Check the status of any convictions you may have. It could be that you don't have to declare them.
- You don't need to mention information such as a disability unless it is likely to affect your work.
- If you decide to include information which you think an employer could use to discriminate against you, try to include it positively, if possible.
- Focus on your strengths, re-ordering the sections of your CV if necessary.

Chapter 10
Matching the Advertisement

Once you have your basic CV, you need to tailor it specifically to suit the job you are applying for. Job advertisements do not just tell you that there is a vacancy in an organisation, they are also full of helpful pointers as to what you should put in your CV, and are a crucial tool in creating an effective CV for the job you are applying for. Using the information contained in the advertisement to your advantage can significantly increase your chances of getting invited to an interview.

Get as much information as you can about the position: read the job advertisement, the job description and person specification if you have them. Highlight key requirements and key words. Make a list of what is required. Then go and check through your CV, making a list of where you match the profile. You can then edit the way you have expressed your attributes in your CV to use the same key words and phrases as you have highlighted in the advertisement.

When you have described clearly the matching information, continue to give all other information relevant to your application. Try not to surround the vital matching information with too much additional information, as it could detract and distract attention from key areas.

Finding additional information

If you write or telephone a company in response to a job advertisement, you could receive an information pack, either before or after you have submitted your CV or application form. Always take advantage of the opportunity to receive one of these packs, before you apply if possible, because they are full of information that will help you put together a much better application and to perform better at the interview. Take full advantage of the information provided and read everything carefully.

The pack is likely to include: the company's mission statement, which will tell you about the company's aims and objectives; the annual report; equal opportunities policy and monitoring form; their policy relating to employing people with a criminal record and spent convictions; medical enquiry form; further details of the job description or person specification.

If nothing else is available, look up the company on the internet and find out as much as you can about the nature of the company and its products and services. Ask for a brochure or catalogue or go into the store in question and have a look around. This will all help you in matching your application to the qualities they want and will prepare you for an interview should you be asked to go, as employers usually ask what a candidate knows about the company they wish to join.

Company information

This is often in the form of the company's annual report, which tells you all about how the company is performing in its chosen sphere of operation, about its key successes during the past year and even its failures, its plans for the future and quite a lot about its 'people' policies and practices. It also gives a lot of financial details such as sources of finance, profit and loss accounts and auditors' reports. It is prepared for the company's shareholders so is designed to be easily understood by the layperson. It is also an invaluable tool when preparing your questions for your interview (see Chapter 17).

Detailed job description

A detailed description of the individual tasks, duties and responsibilities which make up the job is often provided in an information pack, or you can ask for more details, especially if the advertisement did not have much space for specifics. This document can be extremely helpful to you when devising your CV or when completing the company application form. It should tell you more than the advertisement, including who you are accountable to, and frequently specifies the limits of authority of the position.

This an simple example of a job description.

Job Title: Administrative Assistant

Main purpose of the job:
- To provide a competent administrative and clerical support to the caring staff.
- To provide an efficient and friendly response to personal enquiries from members of the general public.
- To maintain and update records accurately.
- To provide a friendly, helpful telephone answering service responding to questions from the public, and other departments, including referring queries to the appropriate person.

Accountable to:
- The Administrator.

Principal responsibilities:
- To provide friendly, helpful reception service for the Trust as designated by the Administrator.
- To provide an accurate, competent administrative support for the Caring Team, as designated by the Administrator.
- To assist with administrative tasks including responding to mail, filing, photocopying, as required by the Administrator.
- To answer the telephone and deal with queries from members of the public, liaising with other personnel as appropriate.
- To undertake the typing of records, letters and documents to the standards set down by the Trust.
- To observe all Health and Safety rules, regulations and procedures as designated by the Trust.
- To undertake any other duties and responsibilities, as may be required by the Trust and its representatives, and for which appropriate training will be given.
- The successful applicant must be prepared to work unsociable hours if required.

Person specification

This a specific description of the person the employer would like to recruit to do the job. The employer will have decided which qualities and abilities the applicant must have or are essential, and which of the qualities and abilities they should have or are desirable. Not every prospective employer will have prepared a person specification, but if they have, it is unlikely that they will recruit without using this standard as a guide. This is another extremely helpful piece of information that can be used to prepare your CV, to fill in the application form, and to prepare your questions and answers for the interview.

Some person specifications are extremely detailed, specifying communication skills and essential or desirable aptitudes. Most employers have a very clear idea of the essential and desirable experience, skill, knowledge and qualifications they are looking for even if it is not on paper, and you may get this information by making a telephone call to the company and asking the appropriate person for their views on the subject. If you are able to get a person specification, whether it is verbal or written, use it to build up your CV or fill in the sections of the application form. The person specification will also help you to prepare for the interview. The interviewers are likely to use it to draw up their shortlist of candidates to interview, and to confirm their decision to make a job offer.

This is an example of a person specification.

Job title: Administrative Assistant

Experience and qualifications
Essential
- Previous experience in an administrative role.
- Experienced in using Word and Excel spreadsheets.
- Previous experience answering the phone and responding to enquires.

Desirable
- RSA II/III Typewriting or NVQ equivalent.

Skills and knowledge
Essential
- Keyboard skills 50 wpm.
- The ability to deal with people effectively, tactfully and efficiently.

Desirable
- An understanding of the caring public service sector.
- Experience of using a multi-extension digital telephone board.

Attributes
Essential
- Accuracy in presentation and content of written work.
- Conscientious and methodical with an eye for detail.
- Good interpersonal skills including helpful telephone manner.

General requirements
Essential
- Professional personal presentation.
- Clear speaking voice.
- Able to work independently or part of the team.

Example CV

This CV has been prepared to match the specifications given in the examples of job description and person specification above.

Job title: Administrative Assistant

Name: Jane Smith

Personal profile

An experienced and computer-literate administrator, who is conscientious and methodical, with an eye for detail and an excellent telephone manner. Experienced in dealing with and resolving customer enquiries whether face to face or on the telephone. An individual with excellent interpersonal skills, able to work independently or as part of a team.

Key skills

- Six years' experience in administrative roles.
- Experienced in using Word and Excel spreadsheets.
- Keyboard skills 50 wpm.
- Experience of using a multi-extension digital telephone board.
- The ability to deal with clients and colleagues politely, effectively, tactfully and efficiently.

Training

Further Education Centre   1996–1998

- NVQ level II Office Administration including RSA stage I and II Keyboard skills.

Career history
Selby and Jones   1998 to date

Clerical Assistant
Clerk Typist

- Typed, filed and mailed letters. Maintained records.
- Received, opened and responded to departmental correspondence.
- Manned the switchboard and undertook general reception duties.
- Operated fax, photocopying Xerox machines and franking machines.

Top tips on matching your CV to the job
- Read the advertisement carefully so you can identify the type of person the employer is looking for and use the specific wording in your CV.
- Get as much information as you can about the company.
- Incorporate the employer's key requirements into your statements.
- Match up the requirements of the job with your skills and achievements.

Chapter 11

Presentation

First impressions count. You wouldn't dream of turning up to an important interview in your old training gear, so don't send off this essential document if it doesn't look its best.

There is a huge advantage in being able to work on a PC which gives you a choice of fonts and styles and allows you to re-organise, draft and re-draft until you get it absolutely right. Use that option!

Once complete, your CV should be no more than two separate sides of A4. This is because too much information will swamp your key points and discourage the reader from reading through it. Remember, however, that too little information won't allow you to present yourself properly.

So far you will have been working on a basic A4 word-processed document on a common word-processing program, such as Word, so that you can easily send your CV as an e-mail attachment, if necessary, and be sure that the employer will be able to access it.

First of all, make sure that you have uniform margins of about 2.5 cm. Then select a clear and classic font in 12pt size and single spacing. It must look professional and be easy to read. Times, Times New Roman, Palatino or Book Antigua are good choices. Never use a script font or anything that looks too much like a display font: it will take up too much room and not give a good impression. Don't use italic for large sections of text: it is not easy to read. You can use a different font for the headings if you wish, but make sure it complements the text font and is not too large. Alternatively, simply use bold and/or a slightly larger size for headings.

Use black ink as it photocopies well and is always clear. Don't be tempted to use coloured inks or fancy graphics as they will only make your application look trivial.

Before you finish, do a final run-through with the spell-check, as you could have introduced an error while you were formatting the document. Then print out a rough copy and check everything: dates, presentation, formatting and spelling. Never rely on spell-check alone!

Print your CV on the best printer you have access to on good-quality white or cream paper. Don't use papers with a background print, fancy edges or pictures down the side. Don't send photocopies unless they are very good reproductions, as photocopies do not send a good message to prospective employers. They give the impression that either you are not truly interested in a particular position, or that you are desperate and are sending your CV to anyone anywhere.

Finally, ask someone else to check over the CV. You will have spent a lot of time working on it and it is easy to miss mistakes.

Top tips on presentation
- Your CV should be no more than two sides of A4 paper.
- Use a clear font in an easy-to-read size.
- Don't use coloured inks, italic fonts or graphics.
- Use the spell-check function but do not rely on it totally.
- Use a good-quality printer and paper in a neutral colour.
- Try to avoid submitting photocopies of your CV.

Chapter 12
Example CVs

This chapter contains a selection of example CVs designed to give you ideas on both content and presentation. Because of the size of the book, some have been presented on more than two pages. You will, of course, not find an example that will be an exact match of your own employment or educational background, but you should find examples that come close to what you want to say about yourself and you can pick and mix different expressions, or simply use them as a guide to get you thinking.

The essential point is that you ensure that you present your information in a positive, logical, concise and easy-to-read manner.

Your first full-time job application

These applications will obviously not contain much in the way of career history so you need to focus on your educational qualifications and also use your temporary or voluntary work and interests to show that you have a good work ethic and are keen and responsible. You can also demonstrate a desire to find out more and gain more experience regarding the job.

Your first full-time job application: example 1

Jane Gooding

Personal Details

Address	42 Berry Close, Broomfield, Berkshire RH5 8YH
Telephone	0118 568 9852
Mobile	07785 125489
E-mail	janegooding@aol.com
Date of birth	20th September 1986
Sex	Female
Other details	Non-smoker, good health

Personal Profile

A hard-working, reliable school leaver with a friendly, outgoing personality, who has work experience in the publishing industry. Quick to learn with good computer skills. I enjoyed the Information Technology course and in particular the desk-top publishing elements of the syllabus. I am now seeking a job which will offer me the opportunity to use and develop my skills.

Education

1999–2003	Newbury Fields School
GCSEs:	Seven, including English (A), Mathematics (A), Information Technology (A), Double Science (BB), Geography (C), History (C)

Work Experience

Summer 2003 Daygood and Franks, Slough
       Editorial Assistant

- Dealt with correspondence, answered the telephone and performed general office duties, for example, photocopying.
- Typed letters and was in charge of filing.
- Organised meetings and took minutes.

Spring 2002 Martin & Co. Ltd, Burnham
       Administration Assistant

- Copy-typed and audio-typed letters and reports.
- Opened, dealt with and filed all correspondence.

Special Skills
- Conversational Spanish.

Interests
Football supporter, swimming

References
Available on request

Your first full-time job application: example 2

KEITH DAY

PERSONAL DETAILS

Address: 56 Brook Street, Whitewater, Surrey WT5 7YH
Telephone: 01254 456985
Mobile: 07790 245213
E-mail: keithday@supanet.com
Date of birth: 03.04.1990

PERSONAL PROFILE

I am practical, self-motivated, hard-working and reliable. I am now
seeking a job or apprenticeship within the construction industry which
will allow me to learn a trade and offer me opportunities for
advancement.

EDUCATION

2002–2006   Kingsmere School, Whitewater, Surrey
GCSEs   English, General Science, Technical Drawing,
              Mathematics

WORK EXPERIENCE

Jan 2005 –   Voluntary work during Saturdays and school
Sept 2006   holidays at a home for the elderly. I assisted
               with serving food, shopping and wheelchair walks for
               the residents.

INTERESTS/OTHER SKILLS

Keeping fit
Member of the Dragon kick boxing club
Provisional Driving Licence

REFEREE

Mrs Farley
Kingsmere School
Whitewater
Surrey
Tel: 01254 803306
(tutor)

Your first full-time job application: example 3

José Barentes

PERSONAL DETAILS

Address:	Flat 9, 3 New Road, Bristol BA7 6HJ
Telephone:	01542 125896
Mobile:	07856 785454
E-mail:	josebarentes@macunlimited.com
Date of birth:	6 January 1988
	Clean driving licence

EDUCATION AND TRAINING:

2004–2006	East Walstead College
	BTEC National Diploma Finance and Business.
	BTEC First Diploma in Business and Finances.
	Courses: Financial Planning and Control, Business Statistics, Accounting Procedures, Business Information Technology, Insurance, Human Resources, Banking, Marketing Processes.
2000–2004 GCSEs	Sommerbrook School
	8 subjects at grades A and B: English Language (A), English Literature (A), Mathematics (A), Double Science (BB), Economics (B), Geography (B), French (B).

WORK EXPERIENCE

2006–Present   Cookson and Sons
Duties included:
- Basic office procedures.
- Assisted with the preparation of the purchase ledger account.

2005–2006   Blue Book Employment Agency
- General office duties including filing, photocopying, dealing with incoming telephone calls, preparing and writing routine correspondence.
- Reconciling invoices, preparing the bought and purchase ledger file, balancing petty cash.

2004–2005   Telmart
- Sales Assistant (part-time), Checkout Operator.

SPECIAL SKILLS

Certificate of Competence in Information Technology (Distinction)
Word processing, Spreadsheets, Powerpoint

INTERESTS

Rugby as a player and spectator, reading, classical music.

References available on request

Your first full-time job application: example 4

MARILYN JOHNSON

Address: 3 Walton Road, Cambridge CM4 6HY
Telephone: 02546 125456
Mobile: 07720 125698
E-mail: mjohnson@hotmail.com
Date of birth: 09.12.1983

PERSONAL PROFILE

A hard-working, self-motivated, recently qualified University graduate with sound verbal and written communication skills and the ability to deal with people effectively and productively. Experienced in collating, recording and accessing data, and writing reports. A conscientious individual who brings a mature and responsible attitude to her work.

CAREER OBJECTIVE

My experiences gained through travelling and coping with various situations and different people has developed my interpersonal skills, and helped build self-reliance and confidence. I would like a position which would allow me to use these skills, within the National Trust, to contribute to promoting our national heritage. I would welcome any training opportunities offered by the Trust.

EDUCATION AND TRAINING

2002–2005   University of Edinburgh
BA (Hons) English Literature and History
Modules: Medieval and Tudor Literature
             The Romantics
             Contemporary Political Issues

1996–2002   Kings School, Cambridge
A Levels: English (A), English Literature (A), History (A)
AS Level: French (B)
GCSEs: French (A*), English (A*), History (A*), English
Literature (A), Biology (B), Geography (B), Art (B),
Chemistry (C), Mathematics (C)
Prefect in Year 12

TEMPORARY EMPLOYMENT

2002–Present   Volunteer for the National Trust
Walsworth House, Richmond
Part time Ticket Sales Officer
Job involves undertaking all duties relevant to the sale of
house visit tickets, including cash handling and
answering customer questions and enquiries.
Distribute publicity information about the Trust, and
promote its aims, to members of the visiting public.

1998–2001   Junior Volunteer for the National Trust
                 Hampton Court
                 Participated in the hidden garden restoration project.
                 Job involved promoting fund raising activities for the
                 project and promoting the project to fellow students and
                 tutors.

SPECIAL SKILLS

Conversational French.
Computer Skills: Word Processing (Word, WordPerfect), Spreadsheets
                  (Excel), PowerPoint.

HOBBIES AND INTERESTS

Travelling (I recently explored Cambodia alone), swimming and yoga.

REFERENCES

Available on request.

CVs for a practical job

Applications for this type of work need to emphasise your ability to do the job competently and to the best of your ability. Your CV should indicate what you do best and confirm that you are personally committed to doing a good job.

The employer will want to know:

- Can you work unsupervised?
- Will you follow instructions?
- Do you have any relevant qualifications?
- Are you self-reliant, flexible and reliable?

Highlight the experience you have gained in each job by detailing your hands-on experience and technical knowledge relevant to the vacancy, your specific skills and responsibilities, relevant courses or qualifications. Always match what you are offering with what they are looking for.

CV for a practical job: example 1

JANIE BOSTON

— ● —

PERSONAL DETAILS

Address:	12 Carlton Avenue, Richmond, Surrey CR8 7HY
Tel:	02356 125986
Mobile:	07793 125693
E-mail:	bostonj@demon.co.uk
Date of birth:	10.06.1977

PERSONAL PROFILE

A trained professional silver-service waitress with excellent customer service skills. Experienced in serving at major corporate events and small informal gatherings. Able to work weekends and public holidays. Reliable and punctual with a friendly, confident manner. Non-smoker.

KEY SKILLS

- Five years' experience in silver-service methods.
- Experienced in dressing tables for special events, for example, weddings, christenings, birthday parties etc.
- Efficient and discreet table service.
- Smart, professional appearance.
- Helpful, friendly manner.

EDUCATION

1990–1993	Richmond High School Five GCSEs including Maths (B), Geography (B), Science (C), English (C) and Food Science (D).

CAREER HISTORY

2001–2004	Catering Agency Placements Ltd Agency Waitress • Serve various menus including five-star banquets with several courses and standard three-course meals.

	• Serve at major corporate events, conferences and private parties of all types and sizes.
	• Dress the tables with appropriate cutlery, glasses, flowers, etc. to suit the occasion.
	• Assist with training new members of staff.

1998–2001   Waterside Restaurant, Richmond
Waitress
- Served standard menus and à la carte menus.
- Promoted 'dish of the day' and seasonal menus.
- Prepared and presented the clients' bills.

1995–1998   Meals on Wheels Service
Home Help/Waitress
- Served meals to elderly and housebound clients
- Assisted with basic chores, shopping, posting letters, etc.
- Provided friendly, daily contact for all clients.

OTHER ACTIVITIES

1993–1995   Leon's Bar, Melbourne, Australia
I spent two years living in Australia and funded the trip by working in this bar.

REFERENCES

Available on request.

CV for a practical job: example 2

JASON JONES

6 Crompton Close, Huntingdon HR8 6JY
Tel: 01963 369864
Mobile: 07734 114568
E-mail: jj99@hotmail.com
Date of birth: 21.03.1982

PERSONAL PROFILE
Capable, quick to learn with a real commitment and interest in animals, their welfare and rehabilitation. Reliable and conscientious with the dedication to offer a high standard of care. An individual who is not afraid of hard work and enjoys working outdoors.

CAREER OBJECTIVE
I am looking for an opportunity to train for a career in animal welfare which will allow me to use my caring skills.

EDUCATION
1994–1998   St Luke's School, Huntingdon
Eight GCSEs (Grades A–C) including:
Geography, Music, Maths, Double Science and Technology.

CAREER HISTORY

2002–2005   Chesslow Residential Home for the Elderly
Carer
Duties and responsibilities include:
- Assisting residents to maintain themselves in a clean and hygienic condition.
- Assisting residents with mobility problems, by using wheelchairs and helping them to sit down or get up.
- Responding to residents' requests to run small errands.
- Caring for the residents by assisting with serving and feeding residents with motility problems.
- Maintaining a friendly and helpful caring manner at all times.

1998–2002   Social Services, Huntingdon
Care Worker
Duties and responsibilities included:
- Cleaning and undertaking light domestic duties for our clients.
- Offering companionship on a daily basis.
- Assisting with the preparation of light meals in the clients' homes.
- Assisting clients with their personal care procedures.

VOLUNTARY WORK

1998–2004   Greenways Pets Rescue Centre

Animal Carer

Duties and responsibilities included:

- Cleaning, feeding and caring for groups of rescued dogs.
- Walking and socialising the dogs to improve their opportunity to be re-homed.
- Assisting the full-time staff with the retraining of animals with problems.
- Responding to questions and enquiries, from the members of the general public, about the animals in my care.

TRAINING

- Basic skills for home visitors course.
- Interpersonal and communication skills course.
- NVQ Level three Care in the Community.
- Behavioural problems in welfare animals course.
- NVQ Level three Animal Care.

References available on request.

CV for a practical job: example 3

WENDY KEBBLE

— • —

Address: 14 Market Street, Worthing, Sussex SX9 7LO
Tel: 01580 696365
Mobile: 07748 968763
Date of birth: 04.10.1978
Other details: Non-smoker, Car owner

PERSONAL PROFILE
A registered qualified Veterinary Nurse trained as an NVQ assessor. Committed to quality animal care with four years' experience in a small animal practice. Confident dealing with clients and responding to questions and concerns in a professional, helpful manner. Able to remain calm and competent in highly demanding situations. Good organisational skills. I am now looking to move from commercial practice into a non-profit-orientated environment, within an animal charity, focused on addressing animal issues.

TRAINING AND EDUCATION
1998–2004 The Royal Veterinary College
BSc (Hons) Veterinary Nursing.
1996–1998 Worthing College
A levels (A grades) in Biology, Chemistry, Maths and Psychology.

1992–1996	St. Mark's Secondary School, Worthing
	10 GCSEs including Latin, History, Geography, Separate
	Sciences and History at Grades A*–B.

CAREER HISTORY

| 1998–2004 | Cartwell Veterinary Practice |
| (Part-time) | Trainee Veterinary Nurse |

Duties and responsibilities include:

- Nursing and caring for sick and injured animals.
- Administering medicines and treatments.
- Dressing the wounds of sick and injured animals.
- Deciding on appropriate feeding regimes for sick animals.
- Ordering and control of the issue of treatment drugs.
- Assisting the Vets in the operating theatre and with administering treatments.
- Advising owners on continuing treatments and administering medication.
- Responding to clients' questions and queries.
- Observing all Health and Safety rules.

VOLUNTARY WORK

1996–1998   Rushside Cat Refuge
Volunteer Animal Carer
Duties and responsibilities included:
- Feeding, cleaning and caring for the sick or injured animals.
- Cleaning animal housing.
- Taking the animals to and from surgery for treatments as required by the Veterinary staff.
- Assisting Veterinary staff, as required, when giving treatments and medicines.

1993–1996   Greens Animal Rescue centre
Volunteer Animal Carer
Duties and responsibilities included:
- Assisting with the rehabilitation of abandoned animals.
- Walking, caring for and feeding the animals.
- Cleaning of the housing areas.
- Dealing with enquiries from the general public.

REFERENCES
Available on request.

CVs for creative jobs

For creative jobs an employer will want to know that you have flair, originality and can deliver your work on time, to a quality standard and professionally presented. Remember to match the key skills, knowledge and experience the employer requires with what you say about yourself, and emphasise your technical and practical competence as well as your creative ability.

For a design-related job, you may want to be more imaginative with your CV presentation to show your style and craft skills. However, make sure you remember the primary purpose of the CV and ensure that it is still accessible.

CV for a creative job: example 1

MICHAEL BARTON
20 Green Road, Windleham, Surrey SW6 5DE
Tel: 01985 765136
Mobile: 07739 629696
E-mail: michael.barton@macunlimited.com
Date of birth: 14.06.1970
Full, clean driving licence

Key Skills
- Experienced at sourcing venues in the UK and overseas.
- Theme events a speciality.
- Able to manage and organise events from planning to completion.
- Experienced in co-ordinating flight reservations, hotel bookings and arranging schedules both nationally and internationally.

Career History

1999–Present   West Coast Entertainments
                    Entertainments Manager

Job entails:

- Planning and organising tourist promotional events.
- Arranging the distribution of publicity leaflets and promotional literature.
- Developing a good working relationship with local business people and sponsors.
- Obtaining the support of local councillors and ensuring they are thoroughly briefed about planned events.
- Management and control of the departmental budget within the guidelines laid down by the local council.
- Organising the teams of volunteer helpers into productive working groups.

1989–1999   W. Drace and Co. Ltd
(1997–1999)   Conference Organiser/Sales Promotion
(1989-1997)   Sales Executive

- Organised the annual themed national sales conference.
- Agreed the theme with the Chief Executive and Sales Director.
- Sourced venues and negotiated deals with the participating venues, hotels, airlines etc.
- Prepared all conference documentation in conjunction with the Chief Executive and the Sales Director.

○ Arranged all necessary audio visual equipment to support presentations.
○ Selected and assembled all visual displays and equipment promoting company products at conferences and promotional events.
○ Represented the company at promotional events within the UK and in Europe.
○ Promoted the company products at home and in Europe.

Training and Education
○ Audio Visual aids. Their use, technical and practical.
○ Desk-top publishing course.
○ Public speaking course.
○ Various product courses.

1986–89	University of Hull
	BA Sociology (2:1)
	Modules: Integration, Immigration, Philosopy.
1980–1986	St. Anne's Comprehensive
1984	3 'A' levels: Psychology (A), English language (A), Classics (A).
1982	9 GCSE's (A-C): including Biology, Maths and Geography.

References available on request

CV for a creative job: example 2

Ray Phillips

Address: 3 Walkers Close, Swanley, Kent CA9 4LE
Tel: 01598 678534
Mobile: 07960 698965
E-mail: raymond.phillips@btinternet.com
Date of birth: 08.12.1971
Car owner with clean driving licence.

TRAINING AND EDUCATION

1990–1993	East Sussex College of Art and Design BTEC Media Studies (Distinction) My BTEC introduced me to various aspects of the media including photo-journalism, editing, camera work and graphics. It was here that my interest in photography and copy-writing began and my final project involved staging and marketing an exhibition of photography.
1984–1990	King Alfred School 3 A levels: History (B), Art History (B) and English (B). 7 GCSEs including English Language, English Literature, Mathematics, History, Art History Grades A–C.

CAREER HISTORY

1999–2005	Jaffers Hypermarkets
	Design Manager
	Design Assistant
	Trainee Design Assistant

* Produced material for company brochures, in-house publicity magazines and promotional events.
* Selected and arranged photo shoots, including location selection.
* Selected artwork appropriate for the publications.
* Consulted with store management and assisted with the selection of products for promotions events.
* Designed and supervised the production of the Annual Report, selecting the artwork and writing copy.
* Co-ordinated the work of the design team.

1997–1999	Design Agency Ltd
	Trainee Graphic Assistant

* Selected and wrote copy for a variety of publications and clients' requirements.
* Assisted in the production of graphic material in consideration of clients' budgets and expectations.

           ❋ Attended briefing meetings with clients to discuss their project and to identify their aims.

1993–1997   Freebe Publications
                Paste-up Artist
                ❋ Selected and produced paste-ups for projects for inclusion in various magazines.
                ❋ Liaised with the editorial department, establishing and incorporating their requirements.

EXPERIENCE OF GRAPHIC PACKAGES

Adobe Illustrator, PhotoShop, QuarkXPress.

INTERESTS

Photography and cricket.

REFERENCES

Mr Clayton (Manager), Jaffers Hypermarkets, Swanley, Kent.
Tel: 01598 604123
Mrs Tilly (Manager), Design Agency Ltd, Bromley, Kent.
Tel: 01689 859762

CV for a creative job: example 3

IAN CAMPBELL

— ● —

PERSONAL DETAILS

Address: The Mount, Cardiff, Wales SW3 8AF
Telephone: 01792 869431
Mobile: 07789 57585
E-mail: ian-campbell@hotmail.com
Date of birth: 09.03.1979

TRAINING AND EDUCATION

1997–2000   Wittle College
BSc (Hons) Landscape Design.
Subjects covered: Contemporary and Historical Design,
Planting, Business Planning.

1991–1997   Craven School
'A' Levels in Computer Science (A), Maths (A)
and English (B).
8 GCSEs including Double Science, Geography,
Information Technology and Maths. Grades A–C.

CAREER HISTORY

2001–Present   MacLays & MacLays, London
Landscape Designer
I am experienced in the planning and development of
council parks, ensuring maximum use of the space
provided while working to a strict budget. My work has
featured at design shows such as the Chelsea Flower
Show and won gold at the London Landscape
Convention in 2000.

HOBBIES

Music and squash.

References available on request

CVs for clerical and administrative jobs

The employer will want to know that you are accurate, reliable, conscientious and methodical, and have the relevant technical skills to do the job. Reassure the prospective employer that you will work well with other members of the department and emphasise the abilities and capabilities that you have which are particularly relevant to the advertised position.

CV for clerical or administrative job: example 1

Myna Jafferie

53 Farington Road, Washington, Norfolk NR7 3TS
Telephone: 01639 646785
Mobile: 07790 379569
E-mail: maddrijafferie@quista.net
Date of birth: 21.01.1959
Other details: Non-smoker

PERSONAL PROFILE

An accurate and methodical accounts clerk with experience in a variety of accounting office procedures including purchase and bought ledgers procedures. Numerate and conscientious with an eye for detail. A helpful and capable individual who is now seeking to utilise such experience and skills in a broader-based post within a busy accounts office.

KEY SKILLS

- Good working knowledge of accounts office procedures.
- Processing invoices and purchase orders.
- Input of data including spreadsheets.
- Recording and processing invoices.
- Answering internal and external telephone enquiries.
- Experienced in using Windows, Word, Excel and Outlook.

EDUCATION

1971–1977   Marsh Lane School, Norfolk
3 A levels in Maths (C), Economics (C) and
Geography (B).
9 GCSEs (grades A–C) including Science,
Geography and Latin.

EMPLOYMENT HISTORY

1998–Present   Faber and Sons, Insurance Brokers, Norwich
Purchase Ledger/Order Clerk
Responsibilities:
- Maintaining purchase ledger records accurately.
- Raising order requisitions and issuing order codes.
- Checking budget availability and obtaining appropriate authorisation.
- Responding to correspondence by composing letters or issuing a standard response.
- General filing duties, photocopying and faxing.

1988–1996	Almand Stores, Norfolk

1988–1996   Almand Stores, Norfolk
             Book Keeper
             Responsibilites included:
             - Recording invoices for sales.
             - Preparing records for submission to the accountant for audit.
             - Maintaining the filing system.

1978–1988   Jamal Markets
(1984–1988) Head of Accounts
(1978–1984) Clerk
             Responsibilities included:
             - Updating spreadsheets.
             - Handling confidential information.

INTERESTS

Raising money for cancer research, playing the harp and participating in the local choir.

REFEREES

Mr Faber (Director), Faber and Sons, Norwich
Tel: 01628 647890
Miss Almand (partner), Almand Stores, Norfolk
Tel: 01639 114205

CV for clerical or administrative job: example 2

JACKIE SELBY

5 Ambleton Close, Westworth, Cambridge CB4 9HS
Telephone: 01793 861432
Mobile: 07795 035266
E-mail: jackie@btinternet.co.uk
Date of birth: 8th October 1984

Personal Profile
An experienced Customer Services Adviser with excellent
interpersonal and administrative skills. Proficient with both
manual and computerised systems, with specific knowledge of
Word software. Experienced in conflict management and in
dealing with a variety of service issues. Enjoys a challenge. Able
to work under pressure and remain good humoured, calm and
helpful at all times.

Education and Training

2004	Completed the ECDL and now proficient in all aspects of Microsoft Windows.
2001–2003	Short courses in the following as organised by the Marston Group:

+ Conflict management.
+ Customer care and service training.
+ Communication skills, written and verbal.
+ Various company systems and procedures.

1997–2001	Marsdene Secondary School
	10 GCSEs, grades A–D including: English Literature, English Language, History and Drama.

Employment History

1996–2005	Marston Supermarkets
	Customer Service Adviser
	Cashier
	Shelf Filler

I am able to give helpful advice on all our products.

I deal with returns and refunds in line with company policy and address customer complaints and problems.

I often have to respond to telephone enquiries and deal with correspondence related to customer service issues.

I am sometimes required to assist with diplaying goods and cashier duties.

Interests

Listening to music and painting.

References available on request.

CV for clerical or administrative job: example 3

JANINE TASSUE

— ● —

Address:	Avril Cottage, Churchdown TG7 2SG
Tel:	01659 378629
Mobile:	07956 679893
E-mail:	janinet77@tiscali.co.uk
Date of birth:	22.03.1967

PERSONAL PROFILE

A highly organised and reliable secretary able to provide competent secretarial support. Experienced in dealing with all correspondence, typing of confidential reports and taking minutes up to and including board level. Loyal and supportive with well-developed interpersonal skills, used to using her own initiative and prioritising a demanding workload.

KEY SKILLS

● Providing efficient and confidential support for a Senior Executive.
● Able to undertake specific projects and see them through to completion.
● Experienced in the preparation of reports and documents for board meetings.
● Experienced in controlling the diary, and in arranging appointments and meetings.
● Excellent word-processing skills.

- Able to produce graphics, pie charts and graphs to illustrate reports. Confident with Microsoft PowerPoint.
- Confident, articulate and well-presented individual.

EDUCATION AND TRAINING

1985	Landsdowne Community College
	Pitman Secretarial Diploma (Honours).
	Course included: Pitman Commercial skills, RSA III Typewriting, RSA III Shorthand.
1983–1985	St Joseph's Sixth Form
	4 A levels in Art, Drama, English Literature and History.
1979–1983	St Joseph's Day School
	O Levels. Six including English Language, English Literature and Mathematics (grades A–C).

EMPLOYMENT HISTORY

1995–2005	Spicer and Co
	Private Secretary/ Personal Assistant to the Marketing Director.

- Provided efficient and confidential support for the Director.
- Undertook specific projects and investigations, preparing a report on the findings.
- Co-ordinated the Director's and departmental diaries.
- Arranged hotel accommodation for staff and visiting clients.
- Composed responses to correspondence for the department and the Director.

- Responded to telephone enquiries from internal and external clients.
- Maintained a good working relationship with all other departments.

1988–1995   Woods and Grimes
             Personal Secretary
- Provided full secretarial support for the department manager.
- Organised meetings, wrote and distributed minutes.
- Compiled monthly statistics.
- Responded to correspondence and enquiries.
- Liaised with other departments for report findings.

1987–1988   Quick Quotes Insurance Co
             Shorthand Typist
- Typed reports, minutes and memos for the Senior Director.

COMPUTER SKILLS
Word, Excel, Access, PowerPoint and Outlook Express.

SECRETARIAL SKILLS
Keyboard 70wpm, Pitman Shorthand 120wpm, Audio typing.

INTERESTS
Travel, reading, amateur dramatics.

REFERENCES
Available on request.

CV for clerical or administrative job: example 4

Muhammed Asha

Personal Details

Address: 7 Larson Close, Bradford BR45 3SP
Telephone: 01596 256795
Mobile: 07965 2969356
E-mail: asham@lineone.net
Date of birth: 01.05.1968
                Car driver with clean licence

Personal Profile

A competent Clerical Assistant, numerate and well organised, with experience of manual and computerised filing systems. A hard-working and trustworthy individual, who remains good tempered under pressure, and is used to prioritising a demanding workload.

Key Skills

- The ability to accurately maintain a high-volume record system, computerised and manual.
- Accuracy and attention to detail in recording new information.
- Ability to prepare statistical analyses and reports.
- Able to deliver a helpful supportive service at all times.
- Experience of manual and computerised systems.

Training and Education

1985–1988   Birkbeck Technology College
             NVQ Administration and Office Skills, which
             included the following modules:
             ● Information and Technology skills.
             ● PowerPoint presentations.
             ● Effective management.

1980–1984   Martinday School
             Five 'O' levels including Maths and History. Grades
             B–C.

Career History

1997–   National Health Trust Royal Infirmary
             Clerical Assistant
             Duties include:
             ● Distributing and retrieving patients' records.
             ● Filing alphabetically and numerically patient's
               medical records.
             ● Accurately updating the records with new
               material as appropriate.
             ● Responding to priority requests from medical
               staff.
             ● Preparing statistical analyses and reports by
               interpreting the records.
             ● Providing an efficient supportive resource for the
               medical staff.

1989–1996	Loucas Motors
	Records Clerk

- Provided administrative support for the Welfare Officer.
- Created, up-dated and filed records.
- Undertook specific projects of a statistical nature for the Personnel department and other departments.
- Communicated effectively with all staff and departments.

Hobbies

Football supporter and reading. Play violin in local orchestra.

Referee

Miss Jones (Senior Clerk), Department of Psychology, Royal Infirmary, Bradford. Tel: 01596 876432.

CVs for sales and marketing positions

For these CVs, the employer will be asking different questions about what you can do. Will this person be able to sell my products and increase the profits of the business? Will they have the commitment, enthusiasm and tenacity to achieve the results I need? Do they have any specific knowledge, technical or practical, relating to my products and services? Will they fit in with the company image and the other members of the department?

These are typical of questions a prospective employer will be asking themselves as they read through CVs and letters of application. If the answer is yes to some, if not all, the questions, then you have increased the odds considerably in your favour of being selected for an interview. So make sure you focus on your professional qualifications and interpersonal skills, rather than detail tasks and responsibilities.

CV for sales or marketing position: example 1

NORMAN HUGHES

Personal Details

Address: 3 Blackthorn Avenue, Fleetwood, Hampshire WH3 9HQ
Telephone: 01698 569452
Mobile: 07702 656923
E-mail: nmhughes60@fsnet.co.uk
Date of birth: 5th December 1972
                Full clean UK driving licence

Personal Profile

A well-presented and proactive sales adviser who gets results. Has consistently met and exceeded sales targets, generating an increase of 10 per cent in sales every year since 1999. Excellent communications and customer service skills which have resulted in a prestigious sales achievement award. Experienced in promoting and selling a range of white goods and domestic products.

Key Achievements

* Promoted profitable products, resulting in increased sales and turnover of profitable items.
* Contributed to an increase in sales of add-on products, including finance packages.
* Demonstrably effective with 'closing the sale' techniques.
* Experienced in selling and advising on finance agreements.
* Gained a thorough knowledge of the products within the department including technical details.

- Resolved customer enquires with good product knowledge and after-sales advice.
- Maintained a good working relationship with support teams.

Education

1989–1990	University College London
	MA Economics: Distinction
	My dissertation dealt with the effects of marketing on the global oil community.
1986–1989	University of Exeter
	BSc Statistics 2:1
1980–1986	Cheshire Comprehensive
1985	A levels: Geography (A), Maths (A), Geology (A).
1983	GCSEs: 10 including History (A), Geography (A) and Art (B).

Career History

1999–2007	Draxon Home Appliances
	Sales Adviser
	Responsibilities include:

- Establishing customer buying intentions.
- Advising customers on their purchases, recommending and promoting options.
- Liaising with the delivery department to service customer delivery requirements.
- Advising customers on financing options.

1997–1999	Direct Sales plc
	Sales Specialist

* Generated sales from cold-call leads and qualified enquiries.
* Increased the conversion rate of cold calls by 60 per cent.
* Sold prestigious kitchen designs, achieving an increase in sales of 35 per cent.
* Advised on and completed finance agreements.

1995–1997	Conservatories Direct
	Sales Executive

* Responded to cold-call leads and qualified enquiries.
* Generated sales resulting in an increase in sales of 45 per cent overall.

1990–1995	Deco Mart
	Salesman

* Promoted and sold DIY products.

Training
Short courses provided by Draxon Home Appliances:
Winning the sales, closing the sales, handling objections.
Various product knowledge courses including Hoover, AGA, etc.

Interests
Collecting military memorabilia.

References
Available on request.

CV for sales or marketing position: example 2

Preeya Khali

PERSONAL DETAILS

Address:	Flat 2, Green Lane, Walsted, London SE7 6SH
Telephone:	020 8465 9523
Mobile:	07793 168953
E-mail:	preeya99@hotmail.com
Date of birth:	18.05.1973

PERSONAL PROFILE

An experienced, highly trained Call Centre Adviser with an excellent telephone manner. Adept at working to add-on sales targets. Enjoys meeting new challenges, has a friendly, helpful manner and is able to remain good humoured whilst under pressure.

KEY ACHIEVEMENTS

- Successfully completed NVQ Selling and Sales course.
- Consistently meets targets relating to call response times.
- Provides a friendly and helpful response to all callers.
- Experienced in promoting promotional products and increasing order value.
- Good data-input skills.
- Excellent telephone manner.

TRAINING AND EDUCATION

1989–1992	Bystock Further Education College
	NVQ Selling and Sales.
	Vocational Training NVQ Office Administration.
1985–1989	Biston School
	6 GCSEs (grades B–C) including Drama, History, Art and French.
	Duke of Edinburgh Silver Award.

CAREER HISTORY

2001–2006   Mail Order Co
Call Centre Adviser
Duties include:
- Providing clients with a fast, effective response to their call.
- Taking orders and verifying the correct catalogue numbers.
- Promoting promotional products.
- Checking delivery schedules.
- Achieving call response quotas.

1996–2001   Universal Foods
Telesales
Duties included:
- Telephoning grocers and supermarkets on a regular basis to take orders.

- Increasing order value through introducing promotional products.
- Consistently achieved and exceeded sales promotional targets.

1992–1996   Windows Direct
Customer Service Adviser
Duties included:
- Qualifying enquiries for representatives.
- Arranging appointments for representatives from enquiries.
- Cold calling to arrange appointments for the sales team.

INTERESTS
Theatre and film.

REFEREE
Mr Call (Supervisor), Mail Order Co. Tel: 020 8643 2121

CV for sales or marketing position: example 3

PAUL WINTERS

The Dell, Harrington Avenue, Rothfield, WT9 3BU
Telephone: 01865 982654
Mobile: 07702 456123
E-mail: paul-winters@btinternet.co.uk
Date of birth: 10.12.1972

EDUCATION AND TRAINING

1994	Wendworth College
	NVQ Media Studies.
	Modules:
	PR, Television and radio influences, Advertising, Journalism, Marketing Strategies.
1991–1994	University of Hull
	BA (Hons) Politics (2:2)
	Subjects covered:
	Communism, International Relations, Democracy and New Labour.
1985–1991	St. Augustin School, Rothfield
	3 'A' levels – English, English Literature and History (grades A–B).
	8 'O' levels including French and Economics.

CAREER HISTORY

2001–2007   Woods Banking
               Marketing Executive

In this position I have achieved the following: devised a two-year marketing strategy; established a marketing database; conducted market research on our relationship with our clients and suppliers; developed a marketing strategy to build on their support; initiated proactive press releases and orchestrated a media campaign to raise the company profile in relation to service and after-sales support.

1998–2001   Marston Motor Group
               Press Officer

I represented the company viewpoint in print, on all issues and newsworthy items; presented the company viewpoint on TV and radio, giving interviews as appropriate; liaised with senior production and human resource management and formulated media strategy.

1995–1998   Saffron Advertising Agency
               Media Assistant

During this time I participated in client briefings, assisted in the formulation of marketing campaigns and negotiated media rates.

KEY SKILLS

- Experienced in conceiving, planning and implementing a media campaign to raise company profiles.
- Able to devise an analysis survey of the target market.
- Able to manage a media account of up to £1m.
- Able to obtain maximum media exposure for minimal outlay with the selective use of press releases.
- Experienced in negotiating media rates.
- Designed the presentation of the award-winning Woods Annual Report.

INTERESTS AND HOBBIES

Motor racing as a spectator and marshal. Public speaking.

REFEREES

Mr Smith (Director), Woods Banking. Tel: 01923 567020.
Mrs Caley (Manager), Rothfield Motor Course. Tel: 01923 560988.

CVs for management jobs

A manager must have the ability to motivate staff, enforce company procedures and processes, be an effective communicator, and be able to do a specific job well. Focus on your key achievements. Companies want managers who are competent and effective, and who make a difference in the performance of the team they lead. For these CVs, emphasise your leadership and motivational abilities, comment on your ability to get results and give examples of problems you have resolved effectively. Highlight any training you have received, your commitment and enthusiasm to do a good job and describe your technical knowledge in relation to the job.

CV for a management job: example 1

JAMES BOSSER

— ● —

PERSONAL DETAILS

Address: 12 Sweet Willow Close, Cambridge CM76 8SK
Telephone: 01548 236469
Mobile: 07705 654987
E-mail: jamestbosser@lineone.net
Date of birth: 10th July 1972

PERSONAL PROFILE

A highly trained and efficient Store Manager who is committed to customer service and experienced in high-volume sales supermarkets. A confident and personable individual who is hard working and trustworthy, and has a demonstrable record in getting results.

KEY SKILLS AND ACHIEVEMENTS
- Five years' experience in high-volume sales supermarkets.
- Improved efficiency by supporting and contributing to the staff training programme resulting in a decrease in customer complaints.
- Effective staff management skills.
- Increased sales turnover by 25 per cent by initiating local marketing incentives.

EDUCATION AND TRAINING
- BTEC HND Food Technology.
- Management course including appraisal techniques.
- Quality control training.
- Profit shrinkage control course.
- Course qualified NEBOSH Health and Safety Officer.

1990–1993	University of Nottingham BA (Hons) Economics (2:1) Subjects covered: Stock Exchange, Investment Banking, Interest Rates.
1988–1990	St David's Sixth Form Community College 4 'A' levels: History (A), Politics (A), Economics (A), Maths (B). Additional achievements: Head boy for the sixth form. Duke of Edinburgh Sports Leader Award.

| 1984–1988 | St David's Secondary School |
| | 10 GCSEs, 8 grade A, 2 grade A*. Subjects include Maths, Geography, History and Technology. |

CAREER HISTORY

| 2000–2006 | Daymax Supermarkets |
| | Supermarket Management |

Responsible for the day-to-day effective management and presentation of the store. Entrusted with overall responsibility for the public restaurant, which seats 200, and the fast-service sandwich bar.

Duties include:
- Preparation and management of budgetary targets.
- Staff motivation and management.
- Customer service.
- Health and Safety.
- Correct compliance with legislative requirements.
- Using well-developed and effective communication skills.

| 1998–2000 | Lipsons Food Markets |
| | Branch Manager |

Duties included:
- Management and control of staff.
- Stock control and stock ordering.
- Health and Safety Officer for the Group.
- Devised and implemented HASAW policies and procedures for the Group.

● Arranged training courses on HASAW for all personnel.
1993–1998   Marzo Supermarkets
                       Assistant Branch Manager, Product Manager
Responsible for:
● Training and Education.
● Health and Safety Course NEBOSH.

Various short courses on:
● Product knowledge.
● HASAW.

ADDITIONAL SKILLS
Conversational German.
Car driver with clean licence.

INTERESTS
Badminton and swimming. Grade 8 violinist.

REFERENCES
Available on request

CV for a management job: example 2

Ali Knight

PERSONAL DETAILS

Address: 2 The Shrubbery, Basingstoke, Hants BS76 9JH
Telephone: 01652 894362
Mobile: 07957 145444
E-mail: alik@btconnectd.com
Date of birth: 02.01.1963

PERSONAL PROFILE

A highly motivated Sales Manager with a proven track record in
leading, managing and training a sales team, and achieving
demonstrable results. An energetic profit-driven professional who is
looking for an opportunity to move into general management where
a background of problem-solving skills would be an advantage.

KEY ACHIEVEMENTS

- Achieved the Matren Equipment Top Salesman 1999 award.
- Promoted to Sales Manager 2001.
- Successfully completed the BTEC National Diploma Sales and
  Marketing course in 2001.
- Conducted an analysis of sales results linked to gross margins.
- Improved customer service resulting in a decrease in customer
  complaints.
- Experienced in setting sales targets, devising effective incentive
  schemes resulting in a 30 per cent increase in sales

- Consistently achieved sales targets, with a personal best performance of a 50 per cent increase in sales.
- Designed and implemented an effective sales incentive scheme, resulting in a measurable increase in sales.
- Devised and delivered training seminars for sales personnel.

TRAINING AND EDUCATION

TACK Sales Management Training Course.
Various product courses.

| 1975–1979 | Basingstoke High School
Ten 'O' levels, grade A–C, including French, Spanish, Maths, Geography and Science. |

CAREER HISTORY

| 1990–2007 | Matren Equipment
Regional Sales Manager
Sales Manager
Salesman
Responsibilities have included:
• Motivating, managing, training and leading the sales team.
• Developing a best-practice policy and procedures to improve customer service, for use by sales and support staff. |

- Increasing the numbers of key accounts by 20 per cent through promotional events.
- Devising and implementing a specific support package for key accounts.

H.M. ARMED FORCES

1980–1990   The Royal Green Jackets
Sergeant
Private
Postings both in the UK and overseas.

ADDITIONAL SKILLS

- Completed the ECDL in 2003. Skills include Word, Excel and PowerPoint.
- Fluent in both German and Italian.
- Clean UK driving licence.

INTERESTS

Sport, in particular marathon running to raise funds for charity.

REFERENCES

Available on request.

CV for a management job: example 3

JUDITH ELVEN

6 East Preston Road, Edinburgh EH5 6DH
Telephone: 01786 545809
Mobile: 07956 523256
E-mail: judith.elven@aol.com
Date of birth: 8.9.1956

Career History

1987–Present   Jordans Antique Firearms Ltd
Financial Controller
Duties include:
- Preparation of the full annual accounts of the company.
- Presentation of the final accounts at the Annual General Meeting.
- Development of a three-year budget plan.
- Allocation and monitoring of individual departmental budgets.
- Development of an effective, easily accessed database.
- Management and allocation of duties of the accounts staff.
- Conducting annual appraisals of the accounts staff.

1984–1987   Prestons
              Accounts Manager
              Responsibilities included:
- Management of the accounts staff.
- Undertaking appraisal and assessment procedures of assets.
- Setting up an asset register.
- Producing cash-flow forecasts, profit and loss projections.

Training
- AIA qualified
- Business Planning
- Investment Strategies
- Public Speaking Course

Education

1975–1978   University of Edinburgh
              BSc (Hons) Class 2:1 Statistics.
1969–1975   St Andrew's Secondary School
              4 Highers (grades A–C): Maths, Further Maths,
              Economics and Psychology.
              11 SG levels (grades A–C). Subjects included
              Home Economics, French and Spanish.

Interests

I am an active member of the New Town Choral Society.

Referees

Mr J. Halls (Accounts Manager), Jordans Antique Firearms,
Glasgow. Tel: 01628 994323.

CVs for applicants returning to work after a break

If you are you re-entering the job market after a significant break, your CV will need to show this and explain why and what you have gained from the break. Remember to keep it positive, don't apologise for the break and highlight the skills you have learnt. Emphasise your reliability and commitment to do a good job and don't tell prospective employers what you haven't done. Similarly don't try to cover up the gap; the employer will only be suspicious. Be honest and put everything you have done and learned in the most positive light.

CV for applicants returning to work after a break: example 1

PAM WINDSOR

'Cobwebs', Paington Road, Southampton, SO2 8HY
Tel: 01628 103698
Mobile: 07795 564626
E-mail: pam.windsor32@aol.com
Date of birth: 21.09.1958
Car owner with full UK driving licence

Personal Profile
A efficient and conscientious individual with good organisational, secretarial and administrative skills. Keen to fit into a clerical role which requires attention to detail and accuracy. Equally at ease with written or computerised record systems. After a period as a full-time mother, I am eager to pursue my career again.

Key Skills
- Good word-processing skills. Proficient in Word, Excel and PowerPoint.
- Experienced in dealing with sensitive information.
- Able to maintain written and computerised records.
- Works well individually or as part of a team.
- Excellent telephone manner.

Career History

1992–2002   Sweetings and Sweetings
             Administrator
- Provided competent, confidential administrative support for the partners.
- Delegated and allocated the workload of two junior clerical staff.
- Responsible for maintaining clients' confidential records.
- Dealt with client telephone enquiries.

1985–1992   Davis and Sons
             Secretary / Administration Officer
- Provided secretarial services for the Director including responding to correspondence and typing reports.
- Arranged all appointments and meetings for the Director.
- Wrote and circulated minutes of meetings.
- Organised travel arrangements and hotel bookings etc for the sales team.
- Maintained the service department diary ensuring that service appointments were correctly logged.

1979–1985   Barton and Co
                 Junior Secretary / Clerk
- Assisted with opening and recording all incoming mail including confidential correspondence.
- Responsible for filing all insurance claims.
- Typed reports and correspondence for the claims adjusters.

Training and Education

1975–1978   Minster College of Further Education.
                 Office Studies. City and Guilds stages 1 and 2.
                 RSA stage 1 and 2 Secretarial Skills.

1970–1975   St Anne's Convent
                 'O' levels: Six including English, English Literature and Maths.

Interests
Keeping fit and DIY.

References
Available on request.

CV for applicants returning to work after a break: example 2

STANLEY WARING

— • —

PERSONAL DETAILS

Address: 3 Wilton Close, Barton on Sea, Norfolk NR76 4GS
Telephone: 0116 587 5623
Mobile: 07706 265875
Date of birth: 4th May 1954

PERSONAL PROFILE

A highly trained sales professional with the ability to grasp and communicate technical product details. A personable, confident individual with an impressive track record in achieving results and capable of making significant contributions to the profitability of a business. Since 1998 I have taken a career break to fulfil my ambition of working in Zambia for the Red Cross, rehabilitating villagers. I now wish to return to the UK to continue my career in sales.

CAREER OBJECTIVE

I am now seeking a position where I can put to good use my twenty years of experience in sales and product promotion. I am eager to demonstrate my ability to maintain a consistently high standard of achievement.

KEY SKILLS
- Excellent communication and interpersonal skills.
- Profit driven with a clear understanding of 'added value' selling.
- Experienced in negotiation techniques and in making technical presentations.

ACHIEVEMENTS
- Took over and revitalised the profitability of the Farriday and Mason accounts, achieving an increase in turnover of 25 per cent.
- Successfully introduced a new product to a national organisation resulting in the largest single order for the product.
- Maintained and frequently exceeded the required profit margins on orders.

CAREER HISTORY
1986–1998   Farriday and Mason
                    Key Account Executive

I was responsible for the introduction and achievement of product sales within a designated area and planned, prepared and delivered sales promotional seminars to all levels of personnel including board level.
I also represented the company at exhibitions and promotions.
I liaised with various sales support departments including product delivery and completed and maintained all records and data as required.

1980–1986   Jessels
             Sales Executive
I successfully increased sales year after year and maintained profit
margins for the product range. I also generated new sales through direct
approach to potential customers.

1978–80   Barton and Day
             Sales Representative
Here I achieved Salesman of the Year award in 1979 for increasing sales
turnover by 15 per cent for their new product range.

WORK-RELATED TRAINING AND SHORT COURSES
- Business appreciation – How money works in the business.
- Public speaking.
- Preparing and Delivering a Successful Presentation.
- Health and Safety at Work.
- Various in-house courses including product knowledge, maintaining
  profit levels, and administrative procedures.

EDUCATION
1976–1977   University of Glasgow
             MA in International Relations (Distinction)
1973–1976   University of Aberdeen
             BA (Hons) in Politics (first)

1967–1973   Rossiters High School
              Highers: Politics, Economics and Sociology.
              'O' levels: Eight, grade A–C.

COMPUTER SKILLS
2004   ECDL. Proficient in Word, Excel, PowerPoint and Access.

OTHER DETAILS
- Clean driving licence.
- Non Smoker.
- Prepared to relocate.

INTERESTS
Fundraising for local good causes, £5000 to date, mainly achieved through donations from local businesses. I also enjoy walking and listening to jazz.

REFERENCES
Available on request.

CV for applicants returning to work after a break: example 3

Harold Davies

PERSONAL DETAILS:

Address: 8 Stratten Close, Bournmouth BM6 2QF
Telephone: 01568 695423
Mobile: 077902 256458
E-mail: haroldrdavies@lineone.net
Date of birth: 04.06.1955

PERSONAL PROFILE

A competent and conscientious storeman, with experience of
warehouse storage methods. Equipped with a good working
knowledge of stock control methods, stock rotation and goods
delivery procedures. A hard-working and reliable individual who
takes a pride in giving an efficient and helpful service to the
customer.

KEY SKILLS

- Experienced in manual and computerised stock control systems.
- Able to use stock control software including preparing
  spreadsheets.
- Course-qualified fork-lift truck driver.
- Adept at sourcing specialist items.
- Adaptable and flexible; a quick learner.

CAREER HISTORY

1987–2001   Thompsons Auto Supplies
Storeman/Warehouse Supervisor
Job entailed:
- Coding and storage of spare parts.
- Checking of goods received against invoices, noting discrepancies.
- Stock inventory and stock taking.
- Assisting with counter sales.
- Sourcing specific items from the appropriate manufacturer.
- Answering queries about the products, from trade and public customers.
- Observing all health and safety rules and regulations.

1978–1987   Collins and Wood
Storeman
- Took orders and assembled goods for delivery to the customer.
- Maintained correct storage conditions.
- Re-ordered as necessary.
- Dealt with telephone questions and queries from customers and other head office departments.
- Department Fire Officer.

TRAINING

	Scalesworth Training Centre
1996	Health and Safety at Work Course.
1986	Fork-lift Truck Operator Certificate.

OTHER DETAILS

After a period of time taken off from work due to an industrial injury, I am now fit and well, ready to return to work.

HOBBIES

Active football supporter. Play the cello in a local orchestra.

REFEREE

Mr Ajax (Warehouse Manager), Thompsons Auto Supplies, Christchurch BH4 5GX. Telephone 01568 212456.

CV for applicants returning to work after a break: example 4

JAMES LAKE

PERSONAL DETAILS

Address: Day Cottage, Kingswood, Oxfordshire OX29 8LV
Tel: 01865 254695
Mobile: 07895 125646
E-mail: jameslake33@hotmail.com
Date of birth: 12th December 1958

PERSONAL PROFILE

An ambitious, highly motivated and professional Human Resources
Manager with a sound general management background. Well versed in
employment law, and trained to use up-to-date recruitment methods,
including physiological aptitude testing methods. An effective
communicator with excellent interpersonal skills and a real commitment
to good practice in human resource development and management. I am
looking to return to work after a career break of two years which saw
me travel across Asia in order to raise funds for cancer research.

KEY ACHIEVEMENTS

- Maintained a thorough working knowledge of UK employment legislation, theory and practice.
- Devised a three-year strategy for Human Resources policies and procedures for all grades of personnel.
- Provided an effective resource on all employment-related issues for the management and staff, offering advice and assistance as necessary.
- Discreetly, effectively and efficiently took responsibility and promoted good practice in all matters relating to employment, assessment, welfare, training and development of all grades of employee.
- Fellow of the Institute of Personnel and Development.
- Qualified in the use of psychometric and profiling tests.

WORK EXPERIENCE

1999–2000   Emirates Medical Facility
              Human Resources Director

I provided an efficient and effective H.R. service and resource for all employees including senior managers in a company of 500 personnel. I also devised, determined and implemented the H.R. policy for the facility whilst managing and leading the H.R. team, which comprised six people. I also maintained an accurate and up-to-date personnel data system and introduced an effective performance-related assessment scheme.

1992–1999   Marshall Warrington and Co.
             Personnel Manager

I was responsible for devising and implementing a three-year H.R. strategy for the company and ensured and maintained employee rights at work in consideration of employment law. I also advised on and responded to developments in employment law, in both practice and theory.

I managed the personnel function including providing a advisory service for off site field operatives.

1984–1992   Havering and Sons
             Personnel and Training Officer

Here, I delivered training seminars and courses on communication and interactive skills.

I also administered and maintained payroll systems, including expenses.

1978–1984   Personnel Officer

My duties included personnel administration including recruitment and selection procedures and payroll.

TRAINING AND EDUCATION

- Fellow of the Institute of Personnel and Development (1995).
- Course-qualified Training Officer (1994).
- Psychometric and Profiling registered user (1984).
- Various management short courses (1978–2000).

1975–1977	South Wales Further Education College
	3 'A' levels in Economics (A), Psychology (B) and Sociology (B).
1971–1975	South Wales Secondary School
	7 'O' levels including Maths, Science and French (grades A–B).

INTERESTS

I enjoy listening to a wide range of music and sing in a band. I am also a keen gardener and enjoy walking.

REFERENCES AVAILABLE ON REQUEST

Chapter 13
The Final Version

You have now prepared your CV, presented it well and refined it to match the job you are applying for. Remember that a CV is not a static document but something you need to keep revising and updating.

Each time you gain a new qualification or broaden your experience, write it on your CV. Each time you apply for a job, go through it again and make sure it is completely up-to-date and cannot be improved further.

Use this checklist to help you double-check the information you have included in your CV and how you have presented it. At all times, keep in mind the purpose of your CV: to give an accurate resumé of your personality and achievements in the best possible light.

Checklist

Is my CV organised in clear and easy-to-read sections? ❏
Is it the right length and in the correct chronological order? ❏
Have I tailored my CV to match the requirements of the job? ❏
Have I described my career-based skills, knowledge, achievements and experience clearly and positively? ❏
Have I included all my educational qualifications, including the more unusual? ❏
Can the prospective employer see at a glance what I have to offer? ❏
Have I used positive language to describe who I am? ❏

Is there any negative or irrelevant information I should delete? ❏
Is the grammar and spelling correct? Have I put it
   through the spell-check and checked it myself? ❏
Is the presentation professional? ❏
Will the employer be encouraged to invite me for an interview? ❏

Keep a print-out of your final CV (as well as a back-up on disk) and take a copy with you to interviews so that you have details, such as dates, should you need to refer to it. It will also make it easier to fill in application forms if you are asked to do so.

When posting your CV, use an A4-sized envelope so you don't have to fold it, and use first-class postage.

Top tips for the final version
- Remember to revise your CV when you gain a new qualification or get promoted.
- Read it through again to check you have portrayed yourself in a dynamic and positive way.
- Post CVs using A4-sized envelopes.

Chapter 14
Covering Letters

Your CV or application form will need an accompanying letter to promote it to the reader and to capture their attention. It should encourage them to read your application with interest. Your accompanying application letter is just as important as your CV or application form and is your first opportunity, in writing, to create a good first impression and to encourage the prospective employer to read your CV and interview you. It's worth spending a little time getting it right.

Your covering letter should be brief and to the point, well laid out and no longer than one page. It should be easy to read and give positive and relevant information about yourself, what you can bring to the job, and your suitability for the role. It must be free from errors and written in clear legible handwriting or typed.

Make sure that you include the name of the job you are applying for and the job reference, and that you address it to the appropriate person, including their title. Always address your covering letter to a named person within the organisation. If you don't have a name, ring up the company switchboard and ask the operator for the name of the Human Resources/ Personnel Manager, General Manager etc. If you are not sure who you should send it to, ask the company switchboard operator for details of the person who normally deals with applications.

The opening sentences

The first few sentences should simply tell people why you are writing to them. Quote the source of your information regarding the vacancy. Use these examples to compose your own letter.

Examples

- I read with interest your advertisement in the *Daily Planet* of 28 November and enclose my CV for your consideration.
- I am pleased to enclose my application for the position of Graduate Trainee as advertised in the *Morning Star* of 29 March.
- I wish to apply for the post of Retail Assistant as advertised in the *Evening Post* of 3 April and enclose my CV for your consideration.
- I read with interest to your advertisement in the *Daily News* and I wish to apply for the post of Plumber's Assistant.

Tell them what you have to offer

In the next paragraph, encourage them to select you for an interview by showing how suitable a candidate you are. Tell them something that will immediately capture their attention and encourage them to read your application with interest.

Focus on the actual wording used in the advertisement so that you can describe your capabilities, experience and key skills in a few sentences which are specifically pertinent to the advertised position. Highlight what you are able to offer and, if it is going to be helpful to your application, tell them how many years you have been in the industry and the position you have reached.

If it is a speculative application, ask for the opportunity of an interview to discuss your application further.

Examples

- I read your advertisement with interest and feel that this position would offer me the opportunity to combine my training and experience for the benefit of your company.

- I am an experienced heating engineer with four years' practical experience within the heating industry working with industrial appliances. This position would offer me the opportunity to maximise my NVQ training and practical experience, and contribute directly to the benefit of the company.

- As you will see from my CV, I am a determined and reliable individual capable of rising to new challenges. My major contribution as a fundraiser for a national charity was a highly successful fundraising campaign, resulting in a consistent flow of income, for the foreseeable future. This post would offer me the opportunity to use these skills to generate income, for a cause I am personally committed to.

- I have been a full-time mother for the last four years. My daughter is now about to start school, and with the support of the local child minder service, I am free and eager to pursue my career once again. I have maintained and updated my word-processing skills by attending courses, and through part-time and volunteer work. I am now looking for a position which would allow me to use my considerable administrative experience, and to prove I can make an effective contribution.

- I have seven good GCSE passes including maths and physics. I am now seeking the opportunity to learn a trade and to prove my commitment to succeed, within a progressive and forward-looking organisation.

- Further to our telephone conversation this morning, I believe that you are looking for a person who brings a high level of achievement and professionalism to their work. I believe that I meet this criteria, and am confident that I could make a significant contribution to your organisation.

End on a positive

Conclude your letter on a positive note with encouragement for further contact.

Examples

- I leave school on 27 July and would be available to start work immediately. I would be grateful for the opportunity to discuss my application further at an interview.
- I would be pleased to supply any further information you may require to support my application, and look forward to hearing from you in the future.
- I would be grateful if you would send me an application form together with information relating to the company and the job, including experience and/or qualifications required.
- I would welcome the opportunity to discuss a possible suitable post with your organisation.
- I am available for interview on most days, subject to reasonable prior notice.
- If you do not have an immediate suitable vacancy, would you kindly retain my application on your files for future reference?

Presentation

There is no hard-and-fast rule on how to lay out a letter, but the examples in this chapter will give you various acceptable options. You should always start with your own details, then the name of the recipient, the address of the company and the date. Note the name of the vacancy, and include any references given in the advertisement.

When you address it to a specific person, sign it 'Yours sincerely'. If you have to address it to 'Dear Sir or Madam' – although this is not the best option – use 'Yours faithfully'.

Always use good-quality, plain white or cream A4 paper, preferably the same as you use for your CV. Select a clear and business-like font – don't use script faces – in a 12pt size. Set up even, fairly wide margins. Print in black only.

Always use the spell-check function, but do not rely on it. They are good at catching common mistakes but you can't rely on a spell-check to do your spelling for you. Be warned by the following sentence – a spell-check would allow this without comment:

● If ewe wood like to sea my CV, I wood bee happy two send it too you're office.

Finally, print out your letter and read it through on hard copy before doing the print-out to send off. Sometimes you will spot an error on paper that you have not seen on screen. Keep a copy for your file.

Address an A4 envelope clearly, or print a label, and post it first class.

Example covering letter

10 Warrington Close
Bridington
Yorkshire
YK90 9YH
01254 125122

Mrs N Gaywood
Human Resources Manager
Foxton Industries
Filey
YK8 7HY

23 March 2006

Dear Mrs Gaywood

Ref No: HE802 – Position of Heating Engineer

I read with interest your advertisement in the *Daily Planet* printed on the 19th February and enclose my CV for your consideration.

Your advertisement emphasised that you are looking for a person who can bring a high level of achievement and professionalism to their work. I believe that I meet this criteria, and am confident that I could make a significant contribution to your organisation.

I have four years' practical experience within the heating industry working with industrial appliances. I have recently successfully completed an engineering BTEC.

This position would offer me the opportunity to maximise my training and practical experience, and contribute directly to the benefit of the company.

I would be pleased to supply any further information you may require to support my application, and look forward to hearing from you in the future.

I am available for interview on most days, subject to reasonable prior notice.

Yours sincerely

David Merton

Top tips for covering letters
- Address your letter to a named person within the organisation.
- Keep it short and to the point, emphasising why you are the ideal candidate for the post.
- Keep re-reading the advertisement so that you use words pertinent to the advertised position.
- Make sure there are no spelling mistakes.
- Send it, unfolded, in an A4 envelope by first-class post with your CV.

Chapter 15

Application Forms and Company Information

Some organisations will ask you to fill in an application form, perhaps in addition to or perhaps instead of asking for a CV. Don't think this means working on your CV is a waste of time. You will need a great deal of the same information, and the purpose of the application form is just the same: to give all the necessary details and to present yourself in the best possible light. You can therefore use the structure, information and presentation you have worked on for your CV in the application form.

The application form may contain a variety of questions that you may not answer in your CV. One additional advantage of an application form for an employer is that the information from each candidate is presented in the same way so that they are easier to compare. The disadvantage is that you can't put in your own spin, as you can on your CV.

Some employers will accept the two documents and, if you have provided a CV, will not expect you to include all the details relating to your job history or educational qualifications on the application form. If that is the case, simply mark the relevant section 'Refer to CV'. Other employers, however, will require the application form to be filled in section by section in detail, even though they already have your CV.

Accuracy of information

Company application forms also contain a statement, which you are required to sign, confirming that all the information you have given on the form is true. They may also contain other statements which you are required to sign, relating to your health. In particular you will be asked whether or not you suffer from any recurring illness, how many days you were absent from work during a given period and so on. Application forms, if you are offered a position, are generally accepted by employers as forming part of your contract with them. Consequently, if they are subsequently found to contain untrue or misleading statements about your background, health or qualifications, it could jeopardise your continued employment with the company.

Basic application form

The purpose of the application form is to give the employer the same information about every applicant. It allows them to ask questions and receive answers about specific areas of interest to them, and avoids the problem of people telling them what they want to tell them, not necessarily what they want to know. All forms will obviously vary in content and presentation but all will allow you space to fill in as much information as the employer needs. The following example should give you a guide on what to expect.

S. SMITH AND CO. LTD

In order to enable us to consider your application, please ensure that you complete all sections of the application form.

Application for the post of:

Personal details

Name: . . . .

Address: . . . .

Postcode: . . . .

Telephone: . . . .

Mobile: . . . .

E-mail: . . . .

Employment history

Name of current/last employer: . . . .

Position held:

Dates of employment: . . . .

Primary responsibilities: . . . .

Reason for leaving: . . . .

Previous employment

Including voluntary work. Start with the most recent and work backwards. Give the reason for leaving at each job change.

Name of employer: . . . .

Position held:

Dates of employment: . . . .

Primary responsibilities: . . . .

Reason for leaving: . . . .

Name of employer: . . . .
Position held:
Dates of employment: . . . .
Primary responsibilities: . . . .
Reason for leaving: . . . .

Education and training
Name of university or college: . . . .
Course of study: . . . .
Dates attended: . . . .
Qualifications gained: . . . .

Name of school: . . . .
Dates attended: . . . .
Qualifications gained: . . . .

Interests and hobbies
Give details of your out-of-work activities and interests.

. . . .
. . . .
. . . .
. . . .
. . . .
. . . .

Additional information to support your application

Your completed application form is an essential part of our selection process. The information you give will enable us to decide whether or not you should be selected and short listed for an interview.

Please use the space below to say what you would contribute to the role.

An information pack is provided for your reference.

. . . .
. . . .
. . . .
. . . .
. . . .
. . . .
. . . .
. . . .
. . . .
. . . .
. . . .
. . . .
. . . .
. . . .

Criminal convictions

Please delete as appropriate

Have you ever been convicted of a criminal offence?   Yes / No

If yes, please give details of convictions current or 'spent', cautions, reprimands and final warnings:

Please refer to the company policy statement attached (see below).

Disability information

Please delete as appropriate

Do you have a disability as defined under the Disability
Discrimination Act 1995?   Yes / No

Do you have any disability which may affect your ability to
do the job?   Yes / No

Are there any adjustments you feel should be made to the
recruitment process to assist you with your application.   Yes / No

If yes, please specify:

References

Please give the names and contact addresses of two referees. Your
present or most recent employer should be included in your selection.

Referee One: . . . .

Name: . . . .

Address: . . . .

. . . .

. . . .

Telephone: . . . .

E-mail: . . . .

Job title: . . . .

Relationship to applicant:

If you do not wish us to approach this referee without your prior
permission, please tick the box.   ❏

Referee Two

Name: . . . .

Address: . . . .

. . . .

. . . .

Telephone: . . . .

E-mail: . . . .

Job title: . . . .

Relationship to applicant: . . . .

If you do not wish us to approach this referee without your prior permission, please tick the box. ❏

I hereby declare that the particulars I have given on this form are correct. I understand that any falsification could give proper cause for dismissal.

Signature. . . . . Date. . . . .

Completed application forms should be sent to:
HR Manager
S. Smith and Co. Ltd
Torrington Road
Brighton
BR1 5EP

To assist us with future job vacancy advertising purposes, please tell us how you heard about this vacancy . . . .

Filling in the application form

Read the form carefully before you start to fill it in and note any special instructions relevant to how you should complete the form. Check, for example, whether you are required to complete the form in block capitals. See whether it asks you to put your surname first – as many forms do – so that you don't fill in the first box wrongly.

Do not fold the form, either prior to completion or after it. Keep it clean and uncreased, and fill it in on a clean flat surface. Use a good black pen as it photocopies better than blue.

Take a photocopy of the application form if you can, and practise on the copy by filling it in first. If there is something on the form that you don't understand, ask someone at the point of completion, or ring up and talk to an appropriate person if you are completing it at home. Decide what you are going to say in response to each section, and make a rough draft of your answer before you start to write.

Have your CV with you so you can make sure that the details you are giving, including dates, are the same on the application form as on your CV. The principles are the same as when you were preparing your CV. You need to read all the information relating to the job very carefully so that you can identify the skills, knowledge, experience and qualifications that make up the selection criteria for the person the employer feels would be most suitable to fill this position – then match your description with these. Pick out words and phrases, and draw them out to compile a statement about your suitability for the job.

Attach a further sheet if you feel it is essential to give more information to support your application. It is quite acceptable to do this with an application form, and quite often an application form carries a statement to that effect.

Respond to every question and every section on the form or mark the question or section N/A (not applicable) if it is not relevant or does not apply to you.

Take a photocopy of the completed form and keep it for your future reference. Do not fold the form, and post it, if possible, in an A4 envelope with your letter of application.

Equal opportunities monitoring form

Companies who operate an equal opportunities policy need to monitor the effectiveness of their policy and will often send a questionnaire with an application form. Completion of the form is not compulsory and it is not signed or dated.

The form should also tell you that the information given will be treated as highly confidential, that it will be kept separate from the application form and will only be used to provide company/organisational statistics, and that the form will then be destroyed. It should not be made available to the people involved in short listing applicants for interview, nor will it be seen by the interviewing panel. To ensure that the form is treated separately, many companies provide a separate envelope appropriately marked. Alternatively you can take the initiative and submit the equal opportunities form in a separate envelope if you wish.

You will be asked to give information as to your ethnic background by ticking the appropriate box. It normally carries a question about your age, sometimes your date of birth, your gender and your marital status. It may also ask if you consider yourself disabled, and will stress that this question is not related to your ability to do the job.

This is an example of an equal opportunities form, although obviously they will vary in content and format.

Please identify the group which you feel most accurately describes you by ticking the appropriate box. Please only tick one box.

- ❏ African
- ❏ Bangladeshi
- ❏ Black British
- ❏ British
- ❏ British African
- ❏ British Asian
- ❏ British Caribbean
- ❏ Caribbean
- ❏ Chinese
- ❏ English
- ❏ Indian
- ❏ Irish
- ❏ Pakistani
- ❏ Scottish
- ❏ Welsh
- ❏ White British
- ❏ Other ethnic background

Age:................ Gender: Male / Female

Marital Status: Married / Single / Divorced

Nationality: . . . .

Medical enquiry form

Enquiries about your general state of health and well-being are part of the selection process and normal practice, as are questions about your absence record. The prospective employer will usually request you to fill in a questionnaire, describing your present state of health, your health history and your sickness record, either as part of the application form or attached to it. The completed form will require your signature on a statement saying that you have disclosed any health problems, and that you understand that any mis-statement or omission may constitute grounds for disciplinary action or result in the termination of your contract immediately, and without notice.

You should be aware that if you are offered a position, it is quite usual for the employer to ask your previous employers, as part of the reference application, for details of your absence record with them.

This example gives you an idea of what you may encounter.

Name . . . .

Address . . . .

Position applied for: . . . .

Are you in good physical health at present?   Yes / No
If no, please give details: . . . .
Are you in good mental health at present?   Yes / No
If no, please give details: . . . .
Are you currently receiving any treatment from a doctor?   Yes / No
If yes, please give details: . . . .
Have you been admitted to hospital for any illness, injury
or surgery during the past three years?   Yes / No
If yes, please give details:. . . . .
Have you been absent from work due to illness during
the last year?   Yes / No
If yes, state how many days. Only include Saturday and
Sunday if they normally form part of your working week. . . . .
Have you any disability, either physical or mental,
which could affect your suitability for this vacancy?   Yes / No
If yes, please give details: . . . .
I declare that I have disclosed the presence of any departure from
good health which may affect the proposed post. I accept that any
mis-statement or omission may constitute grounds for the company to
terminate my appointment without notice.

Signed . . . .   Date . . . .

Criminal convictions

This is an example of a company policy with regard to criminal convictions, which you may find in an information pack.

The Company aims to promote equality of opportunity with the right mix of talent, skill and potential. We welcome applications from diverse candidates.

Because of the nature of the work you are applying for, however, this post is exempt from the provision of Section 4 (2) of the Rehabilitation of Offenders Act 1974 by virtue of the Rehabilitation of Offenders Act 1974 (Exemptions) Order 1975. Applicants are therefore not entitled to withhold information about convictions, which for any other purposes are 'spent', as defined under the provisions of the Act and in the event of employment, any failure to disclose such convictions could result in dismissal or disciplinary action by the company.

Any information given will be completely confidential and will be considered only in relation to an application for the position to which the order applies. Having a 'spent' conviction will not necessarily bar applicants from employment, as the circumstances, background and nature of the offence will be taken into consideration. (Please read our Policy related to employing people with a criminal record which is included in your information pack.)

Top tips for filling in application forms
- Most employers will expect you to fill in all sections of the application form, regardless of whether you have enclosed your CV.
- Write clearly and neatly in black ink.
- Plan out what you are going to write before you start, using a photocopy of the forms if necessary.
- Identify and match the criteria which have a direct bearing on your skill, knowledge, experience and qualifications.
- Match the information with your CV.
- Be clear and straightforward. Avoid ambiguous statements.
- Keep a copy.

Chapter 16
Online Job Applications

With the huge technological advances over the last few years, online advertising and application is obviously increasing. Many employers see the internet as an obvious and helpful resource through which to advertise vacancies and attract a large response from suitable candidates. This trend is expected to increase and there are predictions that by the year 2005, 96 per cent of employers will be using the internet either to advertise job vacancies or for direct recruitment purposes, inviting you to apply online.

It is self-evident that you must be computer literate to access these vacancies – which gives the employer positive information about you – and in many cases it is an appropriate way to apply for jobs.

The most important point here is that you respond to what the employer asks you to do. If the advertisement says: 'Apply in writing with your CV and a letter of application', it does not mean send an e-mail. At the moment, hard copy remains the primary means of application. However, if the advertisement invites you to apply by e-mail, then you must do so. If you are not sure which would be preferable, simply give the company a call and ask.

Online application forms

If there is an online application form, then obviously you will have to follow the designated format. All applications will, therefore, be the same and the format will not allow you flexibility in the presentation of your application, a luxury you have when sending a CV. You may be limited in the space available to describe your experience, ability, skill and knowledge and have to modify your notes accordingly.

The same principles apply to completing an online application form as to filling one in on hard copy, so refer to Chapter 15. Have all your notes, plans and information to hand before you start filling it in. Check each section or page as you proceed, and double-check the form before you finally submit it. If possible, print the form off and practise on a hard copy or save it to your desktop and practise filling it in offline.

Sending your CV

You can send your CV as an attached file with an e-mail, either in addition to the form or with a covering e-mail instead of a letter. Some firms will be cautious about opening attached files, however, because of the constant threat of viruses and bugs, although most firms will have virus protection and will accept your CV by this method.

You could cut and paste your CV into the body of the form if the format allows you to do this, but do be careful about what is likely to happen to the formatting, as it can look fine when it leaves you but lose all its display when it arrives. The recipient should be able to receive your CV in HTML format, which will allow them to receive it as it appears on your word processor, complete with bullet points and border etc. If they can only view e-mail in plain text, it will lose its formatting. If this is the case, you will need to simplify your presentation and simply use capital letters and spacing to format your application.

Remember that a screen is smaller than an A4 page, so think about re-formatting your CV for optimum online presentation.

An accompanying e-mail

An e-mail is a much more informal method of communication than a letter, but you should not make the mistake of sending a short, chatty note reminiscent of something you would dash off to a friend. Don't be tempted to use a first-name salutation; you don't know this person as a friend, you are applying for a job. Below is an example of an inappropriate e-mail.

Hi Sally,
Saw your ad and was mega-impressed! It's really ideal for me,
so I have attached my CV and hope you like it.

Hope to hear from you soon.
Bill Smith

It is imperative that you set your e-mail out neatly and make it professional in terms of both text and presentation. Use a clear, classic font and a legible font size. Use a similar format and wording to the covering letters described in Chapter 14. It does not have to be stuffy or formal, but it does have to be appropriate and professional. Use proper grammatical sentences, and never use abbreviations or text contractions you might use on your mobile. Always make sure that you include your full contact details and always insert a subject, using the job vacancy name.

On page 166 is a far more professional e-mail.

To: Miss S Harper
From: William S Smith
Date: 25 July 2005
Subject: Retail Assistant (Ref 768767)

Dear Miss Harper
In response to your advertisement in yesterday's Evening Post, I would like to express my interest in the position of Retail Assistant with your high-street store.

I am currently working for *Modern Clothes* in Queen Street, where I have been working for two years as a General Sales Adviser. I have undertaken all aspects of shop-floor retail sales and can present excellent references to show the range and quality of my work. I feel I am now ready, however, for increased responsibility and, as a small company, these opportunities are not available within my present firm.

I have taken the liberty of attaching my CV as a Word document. If you require any further information, I will be happy to supply it. My employers are aware that I am applying for positions and are happy to release me for interview at your convenience.

Yours sincerely

William Smith
56 Morcecombe Road, Swinton, Derbyshire SL3 9HL
01254 456952
07985 125698

Checking online applications

Scanners will be used to sift through online applications, and they will be looking for key words relating to the position on offer and searching for a good match with your application. For example, key words which are likely to be matched could be:

- Job title and your description of yourself.
- Specific skills or knowledge.
- Descriptive words such as organised, dynamic, proactive, multi-tasking.

The scanner will also recognise particular phrases relating to experience or ability. Since this is an automated process, it makes sense to be very specific in the words you use and be more careful than ever to tailor your CV to reflect the essential skills and knowledge requirements of the job advertisement, job description and person specification. Use the terminology used by the prospective employer to describe the person they are looking for, to describe your attributes.

Top tips for online applications

- The principles of applying online are just the same as when applying on paper: Prepare, double-check, be focused.
- Follow the same content as you have prepared on your CV, keeping everything targeted to reflect the essential skills and knowledge requirements of the job advertisement, job description and person specification.
- Remember the screen size and present your CV accordingly.
- When e-mailing always fill in the subject line with the job title and reference number.
- Don't be too informal.
- Put your home address and telephone number at the end of your e-mail.
- Read it as if you are the person on the other end, receiving it. Does your completed application encourage the reader to invite you to an interview?

Chapter 17
Interview Technique

An interview has been defined as a conversation with objectives. Your objective is to convince the interviewer that you can do the job, and the interviewer's objective is to find out if you are able to do the job by asking you detailed questions about your past experience, knowledge and achievements and by investigating any gaps or changes in your work pattern. They will also want to find out if you will fit into the environment and the culture of the organisation. Selection interviews are an expensive, time-consuming, basically flawed process for any organisation or business to undertake. To be cost effective they must achieve the main objective and find the right person for the job.

Inevitably there is a degree of subjectivity in the final selection, so in an attempt to eliminate this, the interview is often supported by other selection methods such as aptitude and personality profiling tests, group activities and discussion. Try not to view these processes with trepidation. These tests are not there to catch you out or embarrass you but to give the selection team as much information about you as is possible, in a short period of time, and to help them to decide if you can do the job and whether or not you will fit in with the existing team.

Preparation pays off

Panel interviews are also commonplace, and I have included a section on handling the various selection methods at the end of this chapter. For this section, I have referred to the interviewer in the singular although there may, of course, be more than one.

You spent time preparing your CV and it paid off. You must now do the same for your interview.

The interviewer will certainly be prepared. They will decide where and when they will interview and they will select the format and structure of the interview. They will decide on the questions that they will ask in order to give them as complete a picture as possible of you as a person, and your skills and abilities relevant to the job. In the case of a panel interview, they will decide who will lead the questioning, who will ask a specific type of question, possibly even who will not speak, but will observe. They will re-read your CV and mark relevant sections in your personal profile describing your abilities and job history, and they will design questions to probe your statements and draw out more information about your work background, knowledge and experience.

There are some things you need to know if you are contemplating joining an organisation, and some questions you should ask at an interview to demonstrate that you spent time finding out about the company and the opportunities which may be offered. If you are well prepared you will feel and look more confident on the day.

Find out about the company

Here are some suggestions as to what you should do to find out more about the company. Read the company literature and check out their website. Read a copy of the annual report and accounts. Ask them for a catalogue, brochure, or company information pack.

Think about the following and try to get answers:

- When was the company established? What type of company is it?
- How large is it? How many employees does it have? What are its future plans?
- What is its present turnover and profitability? This information will be very helpful in building a picture of the history and stability of the organisation. If they have had financial problems in the past, it would be acceptable for you to ask for reassurances that they are now on a stable footing.
- Who owns the company? Is it part of a larger group? Does it have subsidiaries?
- What can you find out about the nature of its business, its products or services?

Make a list of further questions you would like answered in order to learn more about the company. Don't ask questions about information you already have.

Know all about the job

Re-read the job description and the person specification and remind yourself of the compatibility of your experience in relation to the requirements of the job. Carefully mark areas you want to know more about, then plan your questions about the job, clarifying specific tasks or responsibilities, training opportunities and opportunities for promotion.

Take a copy of your CV

Make sure you take a copy of your CV, in a neat folder, together with the job description, person specification, your notes with your questions for the interview and a good black pen. Use your CV and these notes to help you fill in any application forms. Keep the information as similar as possible to avoid confusion. If you are requested to fill in an application form, find out whether you are required to give the completed form to the person who gave it to you, or take it into the interview.

Re-read your CV before you go into the interview if you need to refresh your memory regarding dates or other information.

Telephone interviews

Some organisations invite you to ring for an initial discussion and this phrase appears quite often in job advertisements. Treat this invitation to telephone for a discussion as a mini interview. It is your first chance to make a good impression, so don't make it your last. If you sound vague or unprepared, or if you ramble, it may affect the decision to invite you to an interview.

Before you dial, prepare in the same way as you would for a face-to-face interview. Decide what you are going to say and write down key phrases and prompt words. Use the job description and the person specification to emphasise the compatibility of your experience in relation to the requirements of the job. Read again the information provided by the company and prepare the questions you are going to ask the company contact.

Make sure you know the name of the person you are going to speak to, or who will be conducting the interview. Can you pronounce their name correctly? If not, ring up the company switchboard and ask them for the correct pronunciation. And if you do not already have the information, ask for their correct job title.

Make sure that you are in a private place to make the call, free from interruptions and background noise. Keep your questions, and the prompt words about your experience, in front of you when you ring.

During the discussion, tell the person on the other end of the line, in a few short sentences, why you are the right person for the job by making favourable comparisons about your experience in relation to the job requirements.

Conventional interviews

If you have not been told, ring up and ask for clarification concerning the form the interview is going to take. Ask to speak to the Human Resource department, who will be able to advise you on the structure of the interview, i.e. who will be present, is it a discussion or structured in some way? Will it involve some sort of aptitude assessment or tour of the premises, or contact with other staff etc?

If you are required to prepare a presentation, make sure that the appropriate visual aids will be available to assist you.

Always write and confirm that you are able to attend an interview.

Travel expenses are occasionally reimbursed for long-distance travel to an interview. This is usually dependent on the type of job and is best checked out in advance rather than on the day.

What to wear for the interview

It almost goes without saying that your dress should be appropriate to the position you are applying for: business-like and professional for an office appointment, but perhaps more casual for a practical job. Whatever is appropriate, you should be clean, tidy and well groomed. When in doubt, be conservative in what you wear; you want the attention to be on what you are able to bring to the job, not what you are wearing. Do not wear too much perfume or after shave, or too much jewellery. Make sure your shoes are clean and comfortable if you are likely to be shown around the premises. First impressions count. You never get a second chance to make a first impression.

While you wait

Be punctual. The interviewers may keep you waiting if things are not going to schedule, but they will not be impressed if you are late. Therefore, check out the route in advance and allow plenty of time to get there. If disaster strikes and you are delayed, ring at the earliest opportunity and let them know, apologise and give them your new estimated arrival time. Make sure your mobile battery is fully charged and you have plenty of credit.

Always allow yourself enough time to see the interview through to the end, including a tour of the department. Make arrangements to take care of your domestic commitments so you are not under pressure if things run later than you anticipated.

When you do arrive, be aware that interviewers frequently ask reception staff for their first impression of candidates and their behaviour while waiting to be called.

Be polite, even if you are kept waiting. It is not uncommon to be asked by reception to fill in visitor details, or at the request of the interviewers, a company application form. Don't make a fuss and say that they already have this information on your CV, the interviewer will be aware of this when they ask you to fill in the form.

Be composed. You will obviously be nervous but try not to let this show. Don't fidget, pace up and down or fiddle with keys or pens.

Getting it right at the interview

The interview format will be laid down by the employer so you have to follow their cue. Be alert, polite and responsive and you will soon begin to feel more relaxed.

They will be judging your demeanour, so remember to try to stay composed and calm throughout the interview and be polite and friendly to everyone you meet. Offer a firm, confident handshake on arrival and remember to smile – it will help you to relax – and nod as appropriate. Avoid fidgeting, slouching, interrupting and using jargon. Maintain eye contact; look from one person to another when responding to two or more people.

Watch out for defensive body language. Sit comfortably with your hands in your lap. Avoid crossing your arms or crossing and re-crossing your legs.

Put your CV and your notes neatly on your lap or on the table in front of you until you need to refer to them. Accept a cup of tea or coffee only if you are not too nervous and in danger of dropping or spilling it. If you don't have a table, it's best to decline politely.

Think before you answer questions and give clear, concise answers with no waffle. Be confident in what you have to say, speak with enthusiasm and conviction, and give good positive examples to demonstrate how you deal or have dealt with situations or get results.

If the interview is interrupted for some reason, do not look irritated, sigh, stretch or look bored or comment on the interruption. Just stay relaxed and try to look as if you are not listening, resuming your interest in the interview as soon as it restarts.

What sort of questions will I be asked at the interview?

Interviews are about giving and getting information and will only be helpful and informative if the people involved ask the right questions and get pertinent answers.

The questions you will be asked at an interview will be designed to satisfy the interviewer's objectives and will vary greatly depending on the requirements and responsibilities of the job and the skill of the interviewer. You will no doubt be eager to give the interviewers a sense of your capabilities and ask questions. If you don't, you will feel frustrated about the lost opportunity after the interview.

Many questions can be anticipated in advance, and it is sensible to give some thought to your answers before you go to the interview. Most interviewers also have their own special questions which they like to ask and which are difficult to anticipate; just relax and think first, and give straightforward, honest answers. Do not try to avoid the question, as this will be noticed. However, you can reflect back a question by asking for clarification, as this will give you time to think and plan your answer.

Interviewers usually try to ask open questions, designed to encourage you to give a full answer, and you should take the opportunity to divulge as much relevant information as you can. Avoid giving monosyllabic replies. Open questions usually take the form of the following:

● Do you have any experience of …?
● Are you able to offer an example of …?

If you are asked a 'closed' question, take the initiative and give the information you want to get across.

Questions most frequently asked at interview

There will obviously be specific and technical questions related to your capabilities, knowledge, skills, experience and training and its relevance to that particular job. However, here are some questions which are common to most interviews.

About you
● Tell me about yourself.
● How would you describe yourself?
● How would your best friend describe you?

About the vacancy and the company
● Why did you apply for this vacancy?
● What do you know about the vacancy?
● What do you know about the company?
● You have had the opportunity to read the job description/ person specification. Can you tell us where you think your previous experience and the requirements of the job are compatible?

● Why do you want to work for this company?

About your experience and qualities
● What experience do you have which is relevant to this position?
● Why do you want to be considered for this position?
● What are your personal short-/long-term goals and/or objectives?
● What would you bring to this job?
● What do you consider to be your strengths?
● What do you consider to be your weaknesses or areas where you do not feel so confident or would require more training which are relevant to this application?

About your career and ambitions
● Why are you looking to change your job?
● How would your last/present boss describe you?
● What did your last appraisal say about you?
● How would you describe your last appraisal?
● Is it an accurate description? If not, why not?
● What have you gained from your previous work experience?
● You seem to only stay in a job for about two years. Does that mean that we are going to be looking for your replacement, if you are offered the job, in two years?
● What are you looking for in a career?
● What will you do if you don't get this job?
● Why should I appoint you instead of another candidate?

About your education and qualifications
- Why did you choose your degree/university?
- What have you learnt through your degree that is relevant to this application?
- What did you find most challenging about your degree?
- Can you explain to me what your dissertation/research project was about?
- How do you keep up to date with new developments in your field?
- What professional journals do you read and why?
- What recent developments in your discipline have interested you?
- Why didn't you finish your training/course?

About your achievements and personal development
- What is your biggest achievement to date and why?
- What has been your biggest challenge to date and how have you handled it?
- What makes you stand out from the crowd?
- Describe a situation where you worked in a team to achieve a goal.
- Describe how you analysed a complex issue or problem to reach a decision. What steps did you go through and why?
- Describe a situation where you have had to deal positively and effectively with an unexpected or changing situation.
- Give me an example of a time when you achieved a task under a time constraint. How did you react? Were you successful?
- Looking back over your life, what three things have contributed most to your personal development and why?
- What have you accomplished that you are particularly proud of and why?

About you in a work environment

- What kind of work environment are you most comfortable in?
- We have a situation (outlines situation) which the person appointed will be required to tackle. How would you resolve it?
- How would you describe your management skills?
- What methods do you use to motivate staff ?
- What methods do you use to maintain and enforce discipline within your team?
- Have you had to deal with disciplinary issues, and could you give an example?
- Describe a difficult staff management problem that you have resolved, and tell us how you resolved it?
- How do you deal with difficult and aggressive situations? Give an example.
- How do you cope with pressure? Give us an example.
- You have told us that you exceeded your targets. Is that because the targets were set too low?
- This job carries the responsibility for assessing your team. Do you have any experience of or training on assessment methods and techniques?
- Would you be prepared to undertake further training, if it was offered, for this role?
- In what way do you feel you would be able to make a contribution to this job/company?
- After what we have told you, are you still interested in this position?
- What other jobs are you currently applying for?

Tell me about your strengths and weakness

It is almost certain that you will be asked these dreaded questions, so it is important to prepare your answers.

Your strengths should have a proven benefit in your career advancement or work history. Decide on major strengths supported by lesser ones, for example:

- I believe my major strength lies in my problem-solving skills. I do this by identifying the possible causes of the problem by gathering facts and opinions, then assessing the results, and finally focusing on the most efficient way to resolve the problem.

A 'weakness' should always be a strength if you were to look at it from a different prospective. For instance:

- I believe that I am an effective communicator and find it difficult to cope with jargon and double speak.
- I am not good with repetitive mundane tasks; I enjoy being stretched and challenged.
- I have been told by my past boss that I tend to undersell my own abilities, particularly at interviews.
- I would welcome further training in Word to further improve my knowledge/speed/skills.

Tell me about yourself

Interviewers who use phrases such as 'tell me about yourself', 'talk me through your CV' have not really thought through what they want to know from you, so reflect the question back and give yourself time to think, whilst they are clarifying their question. Ask them whether they want you to talk them through your whole work history or whether they would like you to tell them about your present work, reason for leaving, or give them a brief overview of what you have done and are able to do. Clarify what they really want before you answer.

Replying to questions with positive answers

It is not feasible or even desirable to give you pseudo-answers to questions you may get, but a golden rule is that you should always give a positive answer and never undersell yourself. Don't be intimidated, just remember that the interviewers are just trying to find the right person for the job, and you could be that person.

No matter how fed up you are with your present employer, resist the opportunity to make negative comments about them, and avoid running them or your present work down. If it is possible, give your reason for leaving as that you have achieved what you can within your present position, that you are now looking for new opportunities to prove yourself, and that you are seeking new challenges.

If you apply positive thinking to explaining frequent changes in your work pattern, it could help you to explain why you have moved from job to job. In this situation it may be more helpful to your application to condense your work record, explaining that 'between 1997 and 2001 I had a variety of jobs which allowed me to broaden my existing general building skills. I would now value the opportunity to learn a trade/join a progressive apprenticeship scheme/concentrate on developing my carpentry skills'. You can also reflect this approach on your CV or on an application form.

Interviewers with broad questioning techniques or no technique at all

At an interview you have only a relatively short period of time to get information about the job and to give the interviewer positive information about yourself and what you are able to do, but regrettably not all interviewers are competent, and the opportunity to present what you have to offer can be lost.

Some interviewers talk more about themselves and their own success in making their way through life, and/or within the company than about the job. Whilst this may seem an attractive way of passing the interview time as it takes the pressure off you, it is not very productive and not at all helpful to you. The interviewer will not have learnt anything about you, they will not know what you can do or what you can bring to job. It may mean that when you leave the interview room, you will be quickly forgotten, as they have heard nothing that will influence their decision to employ you.

In these circumstances, you may have to take control of the interview in order to give the interviewer crucial information about yourself. You can do this by taking advantage of a pause in their conversational flow and, very politely, interrupting with statements such as:

- It may be helpful to know that I have experience/knowledge of electrics and worked for several months as a senior electrician. Perhaps you would like me to expand on my present duties and responsibilities and how this experience fits with what you are looking for?
- I was lucky enough to have the opportunity of doing my work experience with Spencefirst and was given the responsibility of

organising the rota's for the day and night shifts for 30 staff. I would be happy to answer your questions about the system I used.

- It is interesting to hear that you came up through the shop-floor management route, because that is what I would be aiming at, given the opportunity and training available, in a company of this reputation. In my present post I am responsible for the management and motivation of a team of twelve people, and I have attended several courses on time management, health and safety etc. I am also a course-qualified abrasive wheel instructor and I understand that that is a key requirement for this position.

- I feel that one of my strengths is in problem solving and managing and getting the best from the people in my team. Perhaps you would like to know how I achieve this?

- I am not afraid of hard work, and I have a real pride in a job well done. I am prepared to put in the hours required to finish the job to a high standard. I am happy to work weekends if that is what is required to complete an order.

- I have brought along my portfolio showing details of the campaign/NVQ/graduate project/events experience, perhaps you would like to look through it? May I draw your attention to xxx which was my most challenging and demanding task/project. I would be happy to answer any questions you may have.

- Perhaps you would like me to inform you of my work experience?

A chance to ask questions

At some stage, usually at the end, the interviewers will ask you if you have any questions. Glance at your memory-jogger notes if necessary and ask what appears to be relevant at the time and has not already been covered in the interview. Do not spend ages reading through your questions and ticking off the ones that have already been answered, and don't go over old ground. Always ask at least one or two questions. Speak in a confident, polite manner, without interviewing the interviewer. You can always preface this with, 'I think most of my questions have been answered but I would just like to ask ...'.

Be selective in the questions you choose to ask. Go for quality rather than quantity. A few well-thought-out questions are much better than a large number of irrelevant questions. Too many questions will only succeed in boring the interviewer and encourage them to get rid of you as quickly as possible.

Listen quietly to the answers, and thank the interviewer for their answers, saying that the information has been very helpful and informative.

Leave questions about holidays and perks etc. until you are offered the job. Your offer letter, contract of employment and handbook will tell you all you want to know before you accept the job.

Suitable questions to ask the interviewer

- Who will I be working with?
- Will there be opportunities for training?
- What initial/ introductory training will be given?
- Is the company committed to training and development?
- What areas would you like me to expand on, relative to my experience, capabilities etc?
- Does your company have plans to expand in the future?
- How will my performance be assessed?

- What are the long-term opportunities for promotion and advancement?
- How long has this post been vacant and why?
- How does the department/position fit into the organisational structure?
- Will there further interviews for this position?
- When can I expect to hear from you?
- Ask any specific/technical questions you have, relevant to the various tasks and responsibilities of the job.

Leave a good impression

Be aware of signals indicating that the interview is finishing. The interviewers will close their files and may stand up. They will tell you that they will be in touch and thank you for attending. Do not try to prolong the interview by opening a new line of questioning.

Finally, shake hands when you leave and thank the interviewers for their time.

Be pleasant to all the staff you come into contact with on your way out. If possible, thank the receptionist and say goodbye. Leave people with a pleasant memory of your visit.

Panel interviews

The panel interview is often made up of different grades of people, all of whom are likely to have contact with the person appointed to the post. You should be told in advance if this is going to be the format of the interview, and who will be on the interviewing panel, their names and job titles.

Try to anticipate the questions you may be asked, and by which panellist. Think about and practise your answers. Use the job description and the person specification to draw out likely questions and rehearse your replies.

On the day, maintain eye contact with the person asking the question, but include the rest of the panel with a glance or look. Address your answer to the member of the panel who has put the question to you; do not make the mistake of looking or speaking only to the most senior person on the panel. This has the effect of alienating and diminishing the importance of the other people present and will not be helpful to your application.

Do not be fazed if one member of the panel says nothing but just sits there and observes you. Include them in your eye-contact range and try and ignore the fact that they are not saying anything. They will most likely be observing and listening. The observer will certainly contribute to the discussion at the end of the interview.

Group discussion interviews

This selection method is based around a case study and takes the form of a debate, usually with the other candidates, and is followed by a normal interview. This method is becoming increasingly popular, especially when selecting graduates and making management appointments.

The case study approach is normally based on a hypothetical business problem for which there is no right or wrong answer. You will not have prior knowledge of the topic and almost all of the interviewing panel will act as observers. They are there to assess your general behaviour, your ability to communicate, your contribution to the discussion and how you interact with the group. The case studies are designed to draw out a candidate's problem-solving abilities, the way they approach a problem, their ability to draw out key issues and to demonstrate logic, and occasionally creativity, in finding a solution.

Make sure that you read everything you are given and listen very intently to any instructions. Ensure that you fully understand the objectives of the exercise, and ask the assessment team at the start, whether it is permitted for you to ask questions as you work through the case study, to clarify the situation and help you reach a conclusion. It sometimes is expected that you do this, and is viewed as you using your initiative and all the available resources to find a solution.

Whether you are doing this as an individual or as part of the group, think aloud as you formulate your solutions, and try and be yourself. Do not become over-assertive because you feel it is expected of you, or over-awed by being observed. Even if the discussion is video taped, which can be intimidating at first, you will soon find that you are able to ignore the camera and just get on with the exercise.

It isn't always the person in the chair who gets the job, but it's a good idea, if you feel confident about presenting the group's conclusion, to volunteer to be spokesperson, if one has to be nominated. This is an anchor position, but if this position has already been taken, support the spokesperson by giving your own views and by encouraging your colleagues to contribute, and frequently reminding the group of the objectives of the exercise.

This technique, which is sometimes referred to as gate keeping, ensures that you are taking a pivotal role, while at the same time demonstrating good interpersonal skills, by bring the other delegates into the discussion and by opening the 'gate' for them.

It is usual for one or two representatives of the group to be invited to present the consensus view or solution to the assessment panel, supported by contributions from other members of the team. Always invite questions from the assessors and be prepared to defend the group's solution, either personally or through other members of the discussion group.

If possible, prepare for this type of interview by looking up examples of case studies on the web or in the reference section of the library, and if you can, practise by discussing your analysis of the problem with a tutor, a colleague or careers adviser, until you are more familiar with what is expected.

This form of interview is often accompanied by a social event of some type. It could be a buffet lunch, or taking tea with other staff. Whatever form it takes, be under no illusions, it is all part of the selection process to assess your suitability for the post. You will be observed the whole time. If you read the job description and the person specification before you attended the interview, you will have some idea of the type of person they are looking for. If is part of a graduate intake programme, there may be several vacancies on offer and the opportunity of two or three jobs.

Whatever the eventual decision is, it will prove to be good experience for handling a similar selection processes again.

Open invitation interviews

This method is used when companies have a large number of vacancies to fill. They are informal, relaxed occasions when you are given large quantities of coffee, and background information on the company, including details of the jobs available, to read whilst you wait for an interview slot. As there are no appointments, you just wait for your turn for a short informal interview. If both the candidate and the interviewer want to pursue it further, you will be given an application form, or asked for your CV, and an appointment will be made for you to have a more formal interview at the company's office.

Assessment tests

There are various types of tests which are used to support the interview process, and their primary purpose is to confirm that you are the right person for the job and that you will fit in with the team and the company environment. They will involve you spending time in the appropriate department, or with the team, and at the end of it, everyone who has been in contact with you will be asked to give their views on how you performed allocated tasks and whether or not you fitted in with the team.

Skills and technical knowledge assessments

These tests require you to prove that you are able to complete a required task to prove your skill, for example, a typing test, to confirm your typing speeds, accuracy, and ability to present and lay out a piece of correspondence.

You could be asked to explain how a piece of machinery works, the function of a valve, or what knowledge you have of an appraisal system, and be required to describe a system you have experience of. If you have said that you are able to respond to standard correspondence you may be required to demonstrate your ability by writing letters based on hypothetical situations. Telephonists may be asked to phone in for a chat prior to any interview, or asked to man the company switchboard, so that you can be assessed on how you answer the phone.

If you have applied for practical work such as caring for animals, you may be asked to work alongside another carer to assess how you fit into the team. This type of assessment can last at least half a day and you could be one of two or three applicants who are short listed for the post. You can expect to be given everyday tasks, working alongside a member of staff, and be required to complete them to a company standard.

This type of approach is increasingly favoured by British companies and covers a huge range of jobs. Candidates short listed after an interview can be asked to work unpaid, at a time convenient to the candidate and the employer, for a few hours to enable the prospective employer to observe them in the workplace. This method allows the employed staff to comment on how they feel about having the applicant around, and observe how the applicant completes the task in hand. The decision to make a job offer or reject the applicant is always made after this type of assessment.

Personality profiles

Personality profiles are increasingly used for recruitment purposes, as part of the selection process, and are always teamed with an interview. They are never used in isolation to decide on an applicant's suitability and the results are always discussed with the candidate themselves.

Don't be fazed by them. They are just to assist the prospective employer to be more objective in assessing your suitability for the position. They are a management tool, and contribute to a better understanding of what makes you tick.

They are really a window to illustrate how you view yourself. The way you answer the questions reflects the sort of person you are, and it gives a prospective employer more objective information on which to base their decision. Individual answers to individual questions are not discussed or examined, and you will have only a short time to fill in the form, so just be honest.

Personality profiling can be very helpful in ensuring that an employer gets the right balance of people in the team. For instance too many leaders in a team could be a disaster, as every team needs a balance of skills, including people who are reflective and people who are more practical. Personality profiling is also used in the workplace to form project teams and to help those teams to function and work together by providing a better understanding of each other's contribution.

Belbin Personality Tests are frequently used, and it is important with this profiling method, as with all others, not to try and cheat the test. If you do, you will most likely end up with a very strange profile. The best thing to do is to be honest, as you and the prospective employer both have the same objective, and that is to ensure that you have a happy and productive career with the organisation.

There is a selection of personality tests and self-assessment tools free to view and download on the internet, and I have given you the web address in the reference section (see page 201). Alternatively, you should be able to view them at a reference library.

After the interview

You may be offered the job at the interview, subject to satisfactory references. This may be exactly what you want to hear, in which case, accept subject to their offer being confirmed in writing. However, if after hearing a lot more about the job, you are not too sure whether you want it, don't make any hasty decisions. Thank the company for the job offer, and ask for a little time to think it over.

If you decide not to accept the offer, you must write and tell them, as politely as you can, explaining that you were seeking a more challenging role, or that you wanted to be in a role which would allow you to use your knowledge/skill experience, etc. Organisations, if they have the opportunity, may reconsider their original intention and offer or create an alternative post. Either way, you need to reply in writing, and I have included various example letters in the following chapter.

You may be required to attend a second or even a third interview and there may a delay before you return to the organisation. At each stage, do your homework and go into more depth to find out the information you need.

If you do get to second interview but don't get the job, don't be discouraged. Think of it as good experience and congratulate yourself on how well you have done. It is not unacceptable to ask the company for a few reasons explaining why you were not suitable.

Top tips for interviews
- Be friendly and smile at everyone you meet.
- Give a firm handshake, not a limp one.
- Never have a drink of alcohol to 'steady your nerves'. There is nothing more certain to lose the chance of a job than a smell of alcohol on your breath.
- It's unlikely that you will be able to smoke. Unless it's offered, don't ask.
- Be prepared; it will make all the difference.
- If you know you are going to be nervous, practise with a friend or colleague.
- Think about what you are going to do with your hands – don't fidget.

Chapter 18
The Follow-ups

This chapter includes a selection of sample letters for various situations connected with your application. Always use 'yours sincerely' if you are writing to someone by name, or 'yours faithfully' if you are writing to 'sir or madam'.

Top tips for follow-ups
- Always send a thank-you letter to your interviewer.
- Write promptly to accept or reject a job offer – don't telephone.
- If you are not offered the job, you can write and ask to be considered for any posts that may become available in the future.

Thank-you letters

This may sound odd but it is a good idea to send a thank-you letter to your interviewer as soon as you can after the initial interview has taken place. This helps you stand out from the other candidates who probably haven't sent one, it brings your name to the forefront of the interviewer's mind and proves to them that you genuinely want the job on offer. This is an example of a letter following the initial interview, and before the selection process is complete.

Miss Sarah Manning
4 Station Road
Brighton
Sussex
BR4 9QS
14 November 2005

Mr Stephen Styles
Managing Director
M. Marting and Co. Ltd
Church Road
Brighton,
Sussex BR39 8QT

Dear Mr Styles

RE: Administrative Assistant Vacancy
Thank you for interviewing me on Tuesday the 12th November. I very much enjoyed the opportunity to meet the team and the tour of the premises. I was most impressed by the commitment and professionalism of your staff, and I would like to confirm my interest in position and in joining your company. I am confident that I would be able to contribute to maintaining your high standards.

Thank you again for your time and for considering my application.

Yours sincerely

Sarah Manning

Accepting a job offer

Write promptly as soon as you have received an offer, for example:

Peter Harding
10 Beech Road
Bourne End
Buckinghamshire
HP66 5TG
20 January 2005

Ms Mary Poleton
Human Resources Manager
South Field Pet Foods
South Field Gardens
Marlow
Buckinghamshire
HR8 7HR

Dear Ms Poleton

Re: APPLICATION FOR CLERICAL ASSISTANT. Ref. No. CA460

Thank you for your kind offer of the post of Clerical Assistant with your company.
I am delighted to accept the position and look forward to starting work in the accounts department on 21 February.

Yours sincerely

Peter Harding

Declining a job offer

If you have decided against accepting the post, write a polite letter declining the offer. Respond quickly so that the employer can offer the job to another candidate.

Peter Harding
10 Beech Road
Bourne End
Buckinghamshire
HP66 5TG
20 January 2005

Ms Mary Poleton
Human Resources Manager
South Field Pet Foods
Marlow
Buckinghamshire
HR8 7HR

Dear Ms Poleton

RE: CLERICAL ASSISTANT: REF. NO: CA460

Thank you for your later of 1 January offering me the post of Clerical Assistant. I regret to inform you that I must decline the offer as I have been offered and have accepted an alternative post.
I would like to take this opportunity to thank you for considering my application.

Yours sincerely

Peter Harding

Maybe next time?

If you receive a letter telling you that your application has been unsuccessful but you still want to work for the employer, it is a good idea to let them know that you are disappointed at not being selected, but would like you name kept on file for future vacancies.

Daniella Smith
36 Hamilton Drive
Newcastle under Lyme
NL4 7TH
19 March 2005

Mrs Susan Sharp
The High Street Bookshop
45 High Street
Newcastle under Lyme
NL76 8HY

Dear Mrs Sharp

RE: VACANCY FOR A BOOKSHOP ASSISTANT

Thank you for the opportunity of an interview on Tuesday 10th March and for considering my application. I am naturally disappointed at not being selected for this post. However the whole process allowed me to get to know your organisation better and further confirmed my aim to join you, if possible. Consequently I would be most grateful if you would retain my application in your files for consideration regarding any vacancies in the future.

Thank you once again for your time on Tuesday.

Yours sincerely

Daniella Smith

Standard acknowledgement or rejection letters

Most vacancies attract a high response in terms of applicants for a particular vacancy, and an employer faced with a large volume of career histories to read does not want to have the additional task of having to reply to each one individually, informing the applicant of the status of their application. It is quite usual to resolve this problem by sending out a standard statement or letter with the application form as shown below.

The Rubber Duck Company Ltd
Riverside View
Ipswich
Suffolk
IP46 5UH
29 May 2006

Job Vacancy: Graduate Management Trainee
Reference No: 78675
Closing date for receipt of applications: 31 June 2006
Interviews will be held week commencing 1 August 2006
Venue: HR department

Only candidates who are selected for interview will be contacted again. Consequently if you do not receive an invitation to attend an interview, your application has been unsuccessful.
We would like to take this opportunity to thank you for your application and for your interest in our work. If your application is not successful, we would like to wish you success in your future job search.

Sources of Information

Books

Coomber, Stephen et al, *The Great Adventures Fieldbook: Your Guide to Career Success.*

Deluca, Mathew J, *201 Answers to the Toughest Interview Questions* (Scham)

Humphries, Carolyn, *Really Simple English Grammar: Essentials* (Foulsham)

Smith, Helen, *Letter-writing, e-mails and texting: Essentials* (Foulsham)

Stoyell, Susan and Edwards, Lesleen, *How to write your first CV* (Foulsham)

Yate, Martin John, *Great Answers to Tough Interview Questions* (Kogan Page)

Personality tests and profiles
www.businessballs.com

Recruitment sources online
www. milkround.com
www.graduatebase.com
www.hobsons.co.uk
www.jobshark.co.uk
www.jobsite.co.uk
www.monster.com

www.recruitersonline.com
www.reed.co.uk

National newspapers
Daily Telegraph
All appointments Thursday.
Guardian
Creative, sales, marketing, media, secretarial Monday.
Education Tuesday.
Environment health, housing and public services Wednesday.
Computing, IT, science and technology Thursday.
Commercial graduate Saturday.
Guardian on Sunday
General.
Independent
Computing graduate Monday.
Marketing, media, health and sales Tuesday.
Financial and legal Wednesday.
Graduate public services and general Thursday.
Independent on Sunday
General.
The Times
Legal Tuesday.
Administrative, computing, marketing, media, sales, secretarial
Wednesday.
Administrative, general, public services, secretarial Thursday.
Education Friday.
The Sunday Times
Education, executive, public services.

Local Newspapers
Check directly with the newspaper to find out which day they publish appointments.

Jobcenters
Have a range of jobs and resources available to help you in your job hunt. Ask the staff to help.

Recruitment Agencies
These can be found on most high streets or in the Yellow Pages.

Index